D0784070

Gourmet Glasgow

second helpings

First published 2006
by Black & White Publishing Ltd,
99 Giles Street, Edinburgh EH6 6BZ

ISBN 13 978 1 84502 118 4
ISBN 10 1 84502 118 5

Introduction and establishment profiles © Alan Tomkins 2006
Recipes © the contributing establishments 2006
Food and restaurant photographs © Alan Donaldson 2006

All rights reserved.
No part of this publication may be reproduced, stored in a retrieval
system, or transmitted in any form or by any means, electronic,
mechanical, photocopying, recording or otherwise, without permission in writing from the Publisher.

British Library Cataloguing in publication data: a catalogue record for
this book is available from The British Library.

Printed and bound in Poland
www.polskabook.pl

The editor thanks
Alan Donaldson,
Glasgow City Marketing Bureau,
Morrison Bowmore Distillers, Auchentoshan Whisky,
the chefs and owners of all contributing restaurants,
Rona J Taylor,
www.jonjardine.com
and all at Black & White Publishing

Contents

all recipes serve 4 (unless otherwise stated)

Introduction

Welcome to the second edition of Gourmet Glasgow – the recipe book produced in conjunction with Glasgow Restaurateurs Association and the city's best restaurants. The reaction to the first edition prompted us to publish this second helping with over twenty new restaurants and fifty new recipes, along with four of our favourites from the first edition.

If you're reading this as a native Glaswegian, you will already be anticipating the treat ahead of you; if you are a visitor to the city, you have a culinary feast in store! Glasgow is the envy of many European cities for its amazing and eclectic restaurant and café scene. Add to that great shopping, outstanding Victorian architecture and the plethora of cultural attractions and its easy to see why Glasgow is such a tantalising experience. Indeed, *Frommer's* editor has chosen Glasgow as one of her top ten must-see destinations – the only one in Europe to make it on to the list!

Fifty years ago, it would have been extremely difficult to imagine this industrial city being a trendsetter in European culture and a centre of dining excellence to such an extent that it is now widely acknowledged that Glasgow has the best dining scene in the UK outside of London. The largest city in Scotland certainly provides the dynamic reality of Scotland with Style.

Although it would not be until the late 1970s and early 1980s that things really began to take off, the emergence of the 'new' Glasgow dining scene can be traced back to such glamorous establishments as The Grosvenor in Gordon Street, The Whitehall in Renfield Street and The 1-0-1 and Malmaison in Hope Street.

Luigi, the infamous maître d' at 'The Mal', resplendent in morning coat at lunchtime and full tails with wing collar for dinner, typified the opulence of dining in the forties and fifties. Famous Glasgow stalwarts including, amongst others, The Buttery and Rogano still held sway but generally the choice, for what was only an affluent customer in those days, was still very limited.

Change, however, is always around the corner and along came a certain Mr Reo Stakis who, in a short space of time, transformed the entire ethos of eating out, not only in Glasgow but across the length and breadth of Britain. The Stakis Steakhouses of the late 1960s opened the doors of dining out to a hungry and expectant mass market.

Progress continued into the mid 1970s with the arrival of more 'individually entrepreneurial' establishments such as The Fountain, La Bonne Auberge, Poachers, The Pendulum and The Ubiquitous Chip in the West End and The Colonial and The Duke of Tourraine in the east. There was now no stopping the egg timer of change and arguably more trendy, style bar/restaurants were now appearing. To name a few: Charlie Parkers and The Provencal, Smiths, Gatsby's and Lautrec's Wine Bar & Brasserie in Woodlands Terrace. Sprinkle in the many excellent and diverse international establishments, including La Parmigiana, Ashoka and Amber Regent, and this provided the platform and inspiration for the remarkable dining culture which is available today in Glasgow. These restaurants by no means represent a comprehensive list and readers will undoubtedly have personal favourites and fond memories of other pioneering Glasgow restaurants.

Located within an hours' drive of fresh oysters from Loch Fyne and the grazing glens of Perthshire, Glasgow has some of the world's best produce at its fingertips. The rest of the world clamours to buy, at a premium, Scotch beef, smoked salmon and fresh Atlantic seafood – we have this natural larder on tap. Today Glasgow has the metropolitan feel of a major international city but still retains a sense of village community where local businesses know each other. The restaurateurs in our city all understand that local spirit is a vital factor in presenting a town that is 'together'. Sharing experiences and knowledge is a culture in Glasgow which allows us to progress at a pace that many spectators observe with envy.

It was this spirit of co-operation and progressive thinking that led to the formation of Glasgow Restaurateurs Association. The association has grown over several years from a small number of restaurants to over seventy of the best Glasgow restaurants. All restaurants must fulfil certain exacting criteria and attain specific quality standards to be eligible for membership. Uniquely, the association has allowed a group of widely diverse professionals to exchange ideas with one common aim – to promote the excellence of the Glasgow restaurant landscape on a local, national and international level.

Food and drink take centre stage in Glasgow each summer when the annual Gourmet Glasgow Festival takes place in August. As well as dining offers and special events in restaurants, the city plays host to a weekend of international celebrity chef demonstrations with previous guest presenters including Jean-Christophe Novelli and Antony Worrall Thompson as well as demonstrations from chefs from some of Glasgow's favourite restaurants such as Gamba, Rococo, etain and Papingo.

High standards are expected. High standards are achieved. The famous New York restaurateur, Danny Meyer, President of the Union Square Hospitality Group, said on a recent visit, 'I am enormously impressed with the exceptional quality of restaurants in Glasgow. The commitment to top-flight local ingredients, warm hospitality and compelling design makes me want to return to Glasgow soon!'

With this in mind, how better to share our successful partnership than with discerning diners and aspiring chefs in our own kitchens?

I hope you agree and that you enjoy Glasgow and its food!

Alan Tomkins

Please visit www.bestglasgowrestaurants.com and www.gourmetglasgow.com

YOU'VE ARRIVED.

Glasgow:
Scotland with style®

Auchentoshan

Whisky – Scotland's national drink

For further information please contact the distillery, Auchentoshan distillery, A82 by Dalmuir, Clydebank, Glasgow, G81 4SJ. Tel +44 (0)1389 878 561 www.auchentoshan.com.

With a history stretching back more than 500 years, Scotch whisky sits proudly at the pinnacle of the world's whiskies, with the year 1494 marking the beginning of the journey to the drink which, today is held in such high regard globally. Currently there are just over ninety single malt whisky distilleries in operation in Scotland. Scattered across the four main whisky regions of The Highlands, Speyside, The Lowlands and Islay, each distillery produces their own distinctive and unique single malts ensuring there is a single malt Scotch whisky to suit everyone.

The great variety of flavours which are inherent in Scotland's single malts have traditionally been enjoyed as a dram on their own or perhaps as an aperitif or digestif. However, the diverse characteristics of a malt can make the perfect base for a delicious cocktail or accompaniment to any dinner from shellfish to roast lamb or even chocolate cake. In fact, some of the world's most renowned chefs now recognise Scotland's malts as a valued ingredient, used to subtly enhance the flavours of many dishes.

A great example of a malt which demonstrates this versatility is Auchentoshan. The Glasgow-based malt whisky distillery was established in 1823 and is one of only three remaining working Lowland malt whisky distilleries in Scotland. Auchentoshan, meaning 'Corner of the field' in Gaelic, produces a delicate, smooth and light single malt whisky. The enchanting fresh citrus aromas and sweet, honey flavours are achieved by the unique triple distillation process, whereby the spirit is distilled not twice, as elsewhere in Scotland, but three times which results in a malt whisky with an extremely refined character.

The recipes on pages xii to xvii of this book highlight just some of the exciting cocktails and dishes which can be prepared with Auchentoshan.

If you would like to experience Auchentoshan for yourself and taste the true spirit of Glasgow, then you can visit the distillery which is open seven days a week. Auchentoshan is situated on the A82 only twenty minutes from Glasgow city centre.

Dram'tini

50ml Auchentoshan 10 Years Old
1 barspoon or dstsp Scottish honey
25ml freshly squeezed lemon juice

50ml freshly squeezed
orange juice

Stir the honey into the Auchentoshan in a Boston glass or cocktail shaker.
Add all the other ingredients, fill with ice, shake and double strain.
Serve in a Martini glass.

Auchentoshan Three Wood Sour

35ml Auchentoshan Three Wood Single Malt
12.5ml Grand Marnier
50ml freshly squeezed lemon juice

10ml vanilla sugar*
orange rind

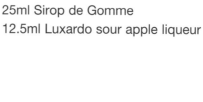

Place all the ingredients in a Boston glass or cocktail shaker.
Shake and double strain over ice cubes.
Garnish with orange rind and serve in an old-fashioned whisky glass.
*Prepare the vanilla sugar by dissolving 2 parts sugar to one part water over a low
heat to form a syrup and then mix in the seeds of one vanilla pod.

Auchentoshan Apple Smash

50ml Auchentoshan Three Wood or 10 Years
 Old Single Malt
12 mint leaves
25ml freshly squeezed lemon juice

25ml Sirop de Gomme
12.5ml Luxardo sour apple liqueur

Combine all ingredients in a Boston glass or cocktail shaker.
Shake with cubed ice for at least 15 seconds and strain.
Serve over crushed ice in an old-fashioned whisky glass and garnish with a mint sprig.

Each recipe makes one cocktail.

Loin of Roast Lamb
with Pickled Walnuts, Shallots and Auchentoshan Three Wood Jus

24 small shallots, peeled
25g butter
3 tbsp redcurrant jelly
2 measures of Auchentoshan Three Wood
  single malt
570ml lamb stock
12 pickled walnuts, quartered

pinch of sugar
4 x 200g loins of lamb with all fat and sinew
  removed
enough vegetable oil for shallow-frying
salt and pepper, to taste
2 further measures of Auchentoshan Three
  Wood Single Malt

Sauté the peeled shallots in the butter until golden brown, place them in an ovenproof dish and cook in a moderate oven (180°C) until softened. Remove and set aside.

For the jus, mix together the redcurrant jelly, two measures of whisky and the lamb stock and bring to the boil. Continue cooking until the liquid has reduced by half and it is thick enough to coat the back of a spoon. Taste the jus and add seasoning if required. Add the softened shallots, the pickled walnuts and a pinch of sugar.

Preheat the oven to 220°C.

Sear the lamb in the vegetable oil in a very hot frying pan until nicely coloured on all sides then roast in the oven for 5–7 minutes. The lamb should be springy to the touch which will ensure it is pink. Cook for a further 5–10 minutes for well done. Remove the lamb and set aside to rest for 5–10 minutes.

While the lamb is resting, reheat the sauce and add the remainder of the whisky. Check that the seasoning and strength of the whisky are fine – if it is too strong continue to cook the sauce for a few more minutes.

To serve, carve the lamb diagonally into thin slices and put them in the middle of a warm plate. Place the shallots evenly around the plate with the quartered walnuts between them, spoon the sauce over and serve.

Iced Auchentoshan Parfait
with Honey, Pinhead Oatmeal and Poached Strawberries.

for the poached strawberries:
200g strawberries
100g castor sugar
juice of 1 lemon

for the parfait:
6 eggs
150g castor sugar

845ml double cream
4 measures Auchentoshan 10 Years Old Single
 Malt
3 tbsp honey
75g toasted pinhead oatmeal
1 terrine or loaf tin
icing sugar, for dusting

Remove the husks from the strawberries, put them in a pan with a tightly fitting lid and add the castor sugar and lemon juice. Place the pan on a low heat and poach lightly for 5–10 minutes, making sure the strawberries keep their shape. Leave the poached strawberries to cool and then refrigerate them for 24 hours.

To make the parfait, using an electric beater, whisk the eggs and sugar together until they are firm, white and frothy. In another bowl, whip the cream until it holds its shape. Add the whisky, honey and pinhead oatmeal then whisk again until almost fully whipped.

Lightly fold the cream into the egg mixture without beating the air out. Now pour this mixture into the terrine dish or loaf tin and freeze for at least 24 hours until set.

To serve, cut the parfait into four 3cm slices and cut each one diagonally to make two triangles. Place two triangles in the centre of each plate with a tablespoon of the poached strawberries. Dust with icing sugar and serve.

Supreme of Guinea Fowl

with Smoked Cheese Mousseline, Jerusalem Artichoke and Potato Rösti and a Sweet Pepper Coulis

4 supremes of guinea fowl, trimmed and with
  fillets separated
1 egg
165ml double cream
200g smoked cheese, diced

1 large potato, peeled and cooked
105g washed Jerusalem artichokes
4 red peppers, peeled and seeds removed
275ml chicken stock
salt and pepper, to taste

Preheat oven to 170°C.

To make the mousseline, purée the guinea fowl fillets, combine them with the egg and half of the cream and add the seasoning and the diced smoked cheese. Put the mixture in the fridge for approximately 30 minutes.

Using a sharp knife form a pocket in each of the guinea fowl breasts and stuff them with the chilled mousseline.

To make the potato rösti, grate the potato, finely chop the artichokes and liberally season both with salt and pepper. Press everything together to remove any excess moisture and put the mixture into 4 moulds.

Put the guinea fowl into a preheated pan, skin side down and cook for 2–3 minutes then turn. Remove them from the pan, transfer to a roasting tray and cook them in the oven for 10–12 minutes.

Put the potato rösti in the same pan the guinea fowl were in and cook for 4–5 minutes on each side, until golden brown.

To make the sweet pepper coulis, chop the peppers, put them in a pan with the chicken stock, bring to the boil and reduce by a third. Add the remaining cream and return to the boil then liquidise the sauce.

To serve, place the potato rösti on the plate, place the guinea fowl on top and drizzle the coulis around the outside of the plate.

Summer Fruits Set in a Sauterne Jelly
with a Raspberry Coulis

275ml sauterne or other sweet wine
110g castor sugar
2 leaves of gelatine
2 vanilla pods

a mixture of raspberries, blueberries,
  strawberries and blackberries – a handful of
  each
1 punnet of raspberries
castor sugar, to taste

Heat the wine, castor sugar and split vanilla pods in a small saucepan until the sugar is dissolved. Discard the vanilla pods.

Soak the gelatine leaves in warm water, squeeze out the excess moisture and then add the gelatine to the wine and castor sugar mixture.

Place the fruit into moulds (either one large mould or 4 individual ones) and pour in most of the wine mixture.

Once the wine has cooled place weights on top of the moulds and press until set. Remove the weights and add the remaining liquid to fill any indentations that may have appeared. Put moulds in the fridge and leave the jelly to set for 4 hours.

Purée the raspberries and add sugar to taste to make a coulis.

Remove the jelly from the mould and serve with the coulis.

78 st vincent

78 is an established award-winning city-centre restaurant. Its elegant warm atmosphere makes it the kind of place you don't want to leave. And taking a seat in the comfortable, secluded lounge area after a delicious meal will make this even harder. When it comes to the food, keeping it simple is the motto here – the chef uses the very best Scottish produce, treats it with care to extract its fullest flavour and presents it with flair and style.

arisaig

Inspired by childhood holidays to the west coast village of the same name, Arisaig restaurant offers the best of Scottish cuisine in a relaxed atmosphere with friendly service. The menu is divided into 'The Land' and 'The Sea'. The freshest of Scottish ingredients are used, including Stornoway black pudding, Shetland monkfish, South Uist smoked salmon and Buccleuch beef, as well as some long-forgotten ingredients such as kale and cairgein.

Roast Monkfish
with Mussel Mash and Red Pepper Sauce

for the monkfish stock:

500g monkfish bones
150ml dry white wine
300ml water
2 cloves of garlic, chopped
1 medium leek, chopped
300ml double cream
50g unsalted butter
1 tbsp tomato purée
100g kombu seaweed
5 small chives
juice of 1 lemon
12 whole mussels, in shells
10 rocket salad leaves

4 medium red peppers, seeds removed
sea salt and cracked black pepper, to taste
50ml extra virgin olive oil
a dash of balsamic vinegar
1 clove of garlic, chopped
a pinch of kombu seaweed
10 rocket salad leaves
500g potatoes
4 monkfish tails, weighing 175g–200g each
juice of 2 lemons
some kail, chives, dulse seaweed and lemon
  wedges, to serve

First prepare the fish stock by mixing the first eleven of the ingredients listed for the stock in a large pot, bringing it to the boil and simmering slowly for 15–25 minutes until reduced by a third. Sieve and set the liquid aside.

Cut the red peppers in half, season and slowly roast them in a little olive oil, adding a dash of balsamic vinegar and the crushed garlic, for 45 minutes. Blend the peppers with 2–3 tablespoons of the fish stock and 3 tablespoons of olive oil. Then add the kombu seaweed and rocket and stir together.

Boil the potatoes in some of the fish stock until just tender, set aside. Then use the same stock to cook the mussels by boiling for 4–5 minutes. Mash the cooked potatoes and add 4–5 of the cooked mussels (removed from their shells) together with 2 tablespoons of the red pepper sauce (which should still be slightly warm). Mash together till smooth. The red pepper sauce will add colour to the mash while the mussels will give a marbled appearance and texture.

To make the sauce combine the remaining fish stock and the remaining red pepper sauce with the rest of the mussels (this time still in their shells).

Squeeze the lemon juice over the monkfish tails and roast at 200°C or grill under a high heat for 5–6 minutes each side until fluffy and relatively firm.

To serve, place the fish on or beside the mussel mash and add the sauce, containing the mussels in their shells, to the side of the dish. Garnish with kail, chives, dulse seaweed and a wedge of lemon.

Chicken Jaipuri

3 large onions
275ml mustard oil
1 level tsp cumin
60g ginger purée
20g garlic purée
30g salt
1 tsp chilli powder
4 green chillies, chopped
1 tsp turmeric
2 tbsp tomato purée

1kg chicken fillets, chopped
2 tbsp ready-made tandoori paste (available in
   most Asian stores and some supermarkets)
550ml water
3 bell peppers of various colours, for
   presentation
2 tbsp vegetable oil
2 tbsp coconut cream
pinch of dried fenugreek
sprinkling of fresh coriander

Chop up 2 of the onions. Heat the mustard oil in a frying pan and lightly fry the onions until golden. Add the cumin, ginger purée and garlic purée and stir for 2 minutes before adding the salt, chilli powder, chopped green chillies, turmeric and tomato purée. Continue to stir until all the ingredients have been blended together.

Add the chopped chicken fillets and mix well. Continue to stir-fry until the chicken fillets are sealed and then blend in the tandoori paste. Add the water and simmer for about 5–10 minutes until the chicken is tender.

Meanwhile, chop the peppers and the remaining onion, lightly fry them in the vegetable oil until al dente. Remove the pan from the heat but keep warm.

Now slowly add the coconut cream to the chicken and stir for 1 minute. Add the fried peppers and onion and stir again. Garnish with a sprinkling of dried fenugreek and fresh coriander and serve.

Chicken Tikka Masala

120ml vegetable oil
1 large onion, finely diced and divided into 2
  equal lots
1½ tbsp cumin
1½ tbsp salt
4 tbsp fresh ginger, crushed
2 level tbsp fresh garlic, crushed
1½ tsp turmeric
1½ tsp curry powder
2 tsp chilli powder
pinch of dried fenugreek

2 tbsp tomato purée
800g chicken fillets
135ml water
1 large green pepper, diced
1 tsp ready-made tandoori paste (available from
  most Asian stores and some supermarkets)
250ml yoghurt
1 tbsp coconut cream
1 heaped tsp ready-made mint sauce
1 bunch of fresh coriander, roughly chopped

Heat the oil in a deep pan over a moderate heat and add one lot of diced onion together with the cumin and salt. Stir until the onions are golden brown and then add the ginger and garlic, blending well. Add all the remaining spices and the tomato purée, stir well and let this simmer on a low heat for 5 minutes.

Add the chicken pieces and mix well. Stir in the water, put a lid on the pan and simmer on a low heat for around 15 minutes, until the chicken is cooked through.

Add the remaining onions, together with the diced pepper, tandoori paste and yoghurt and replace the lid again. Let this simmer for another 5–10 minutes until the peppers are al dente. Now add the coconut cream and the mint sauce, stir well and allow to simmer for a further 30 seconds

To garnish, sprinkle the dish with the coriander. Your mouth-watering masala is now ready to serve.

ashoka ashton lane

Take a saunter down the cobbled stones of Ashton Lane, just off bustling Byres Road. At the top of the lane, stop. Close your eyes, inhale deeply and breathe in the buzz of Glasgow's cosmopolitan West End. The magical milieu is almost tangible and you won't be able to resist the intoxicating aroma of all things spicy, enticing you into the Ashoka Ashton Lane. Is it a brasserie? Perhaps. Is it a bistro? Could be. Whatever it is, one thing's for sure – this bijou eatery is definitely not just another Indian restaurant!

aurora

Aurora's menu has been created with quality ingredients and sumptuous flavours. Inspired by the intimate, warm atmosphere, the dishes are inviting, satisfying and stimulating. Relax and enjoy contemporary Scottish cuisine. All the food is cooked to order and delivered by excellent service staff who not only have excellent knowledge of the range of dishes but also of the magnificent and extensive wine list. Aurora truly is a hidden gem within the city, ideally located for those who want to combine their visit to the restaurant with going to the cinema, theatre or Glasgow Royal Concert Hall.

Craig Dunn

Lamb Wellington
with Mint Chutney

for the mint chutney
1 10cm cube of white bread
80ml white wine vinegar
4 fresh chillies
200g mint leaves
100g spring onions
1 ice cube
200g sugar
salt and pepper, to taste

for the lamb Wellington (per portion)
190g saddle of lamb
salt and pepper, to taste
30ml olive oil
100g mushrooms
120g Parma ham
180g puff pastry
1 egg yolk, beaten

First make the mint chutney. Soak the bread cube in some water for 30 seconds, drain and squeeze out any excess moisture.

Using a blender, mix together the soaked bread cube, vinegar, chillies, mint leaves, spring onions, ice cube, sugar and salt and pepper and purée until smooth. Adjust the seasoning to taste.

Transfer the chutney to a container and chill in the refrigerator until ready to use.

Trim the lamb fillet and season with salt and pepper. Then seal the meat by sautéing it in half the olive oil in a frying pan for a few minutes on each side. Remove the meat from the pan and allow it to cool.

Process the mushrooms in a blender and fry them in the remaining olive oil on a medium heat until all the moisture from the mushrooms has evaporated. Lay the cooked blended mushrooms on a tray and allow them to cool.

Lay out a sheet of cling film, place the slices of Parma ham side by side on it and then spread the mushroom mixture evenly on top of the ham. Place the lamb fillet on top and gently lift the cling film and roll it over the lamb fillet so that the mushroom and Parma ham slices completely cover the lamb. Gently twist the ends of the cling film together and place the wrapped lamb in the fridge for 1 hour. Remove it and carefully peel off the cling film.

Roll out the puff pastry to a thickness of 3mm. Put the lamb in the centre of the pastry, brush the edges with the beaten egg yolk and fold the pastry over the lamb to make a parcel.

Preheat the oven to 220°C.

Bake the lamb in the oven for 20–25 minutes. Carve and serve with the mint chutney.

Pan-fried Fillet of Halibut
on Roast Potatoes with a Coriander and Walnut Dressing, Served with a Tahini Yogurt

30g natural yogurt

juice of ½ lemon

1 tsp tahini paste

salt and pepper, to taste

50g walnuts, chopped and lightly toasted

2 red chillies, seeds removed and finely
  chopped

50g red onion, finely chopped

30g fresh coriander, coarsely chopped

50ml French dressing or vinaigrette

salt and pepper, to taste

500g baby roasting potatoes

a handful of baby spinach leaves

4 x 180g fresh halibut fillets

salt and pepper to taste

enough olive oil for shallow-frying

25g butter

First make the tahini yogurt. Mix the yogurt, lemon juice and tahini together until they are all well combined. Season to taste and set aside.

Next make the dressing. Mix the walnuts, chillies, red onion and coriander into the French dressing or vinaigrette until everything is well combined. Season to taste and set aside.

Parboil the potatoes, allow them to cool and then halve them. Roast them in a hot oven (220°C) until golden brown. Add the spinach to the potatoes at the last minute, just prior to serving, allowing it to wilt.

Season the halibut fillets with salt and pepper and place in a non-stick pan with a little olive oil. Fry for 3–4 minutes on each side until golden brown, adding the butter at the last moment.

To serve, put the potatoes on a plate with a halibut fillet on top of them, spoon over a generous amount of the walnut and coriander dressing and drizzle with the tahini yogurt.

baby grand west end

Baby Grand West End, Byres Road, is one of the
newcomers to Glasgow's West End restaurant scene
but it has already built an impressive reputation. A
stylish interior provides the backdrop to some of the
best food in the city. The live piano music and
intimate atmosphere add to the ambience and, during
the summer, the doors are opened to create a bright
and airy space – very continental.

barca tapas

A unique and authentic tapas and a cava cocktail bar, Barca Tapas and Cava Bar is a new experience for Glaswegians. Inspired by Barcelona's famous tapas bars, Barca offers an ever-changing menu of forty-plus different tapas dishes to tempt every palate and there is an exciting selection of Spanish wines. Here you'll also find the city's only cava bar.

Brema de Mar Estofado

4 x 450g whole sea bream
salt and black pepper, to taste
8 tbsp olive oil
1 Spanish onion
2 sticks of celery
1 fennel bulb
1 leek, white part only

1 yellow pepper
3 sweet potatoes
16 tbsp fish stock
2 limes, each cut into 4 wedges
a little olive oil
12 small sprigs of rosemary, to garnish

Score each sea bream with a sharp knife, making three lines on each side. Rub the fish with salt and black pepper and preheat a pan with 6 tablespoons of the olive oil. Put the fish in the hot pan and cook for 3 minutes on each side to brown. Remove the fish from pan and set them aside.

Roughly chop all the vegetables into approximately 2.5cm dice, add these to the pan and lightly fry. Season and then add the fish stock.

Now place the fried sea bream on top of the vegetables, cover the pan with a lid and roast them in the oven at 180ºC for 14 minutes.

Caramelise the lime wedges by slowly roasting them in the olive oil.

To serve, divide the vegetables between 4 ceramic tiles or plates, put the sea bream on top, add the caramelised lime wedges and drizzle over the remaining olive oil to lightly glaze the fish. Garnish by placing the sprigs of rosemary into the scores on the fish.

Posh Fish Pie
with Cheesy Mash and Buttered Sugar Snap Peas

1 small white onion, diced
½ a head of fennel, diced
1 leek, diced
2 sticks of celery, diced
50ml olive oil
50g unsalted butter
200g monkfish, diced
200g king scallops, halved
200g organic salmon fillet, diced
200g raw tiger prawns

100ml white wine
300ml double cream
25g fresh dill, chopped
25g fresh parsley, chopped
salt and pepper, to taste
500g Maris Piper potatoes, peeled, boiled and
   mashed
200g Isle of Mull cheddar, grated
400g sugar snap peas
25g butter

Gently cook all the diced vegetables in the olive oil and unsalted butter until soft. Add in all the fish and the white wine and continue to cook for 2 minutes.

Add the cream and reduce slightly. Finish by adding the dill and parsley. Season to taste and then tip everything into a warm pie dish.

Make the cheesy mash by combining the mashed potatoes and grated cheese. Put the mixture into a piping bag, pipe the mash over the pie filling and grill under a moderate heat until the top is golden brown.

Steam the sugar snap peas for 4–5 minutes. Put them into a serving dish and allow the butter to melt over them.

Serve the pie in the middle of the table accompanied by hot buttered sugar snap peas.

Bluu's first Scottish venture is situated on the corner of Albion Street and Trongate, in the heart of the Merchant City. Its reputation is built on serving top-quality food and drink and providing excellent presentation and service. There are three distinct areas: a ground-floor bar serving premium beers, wines, spirits and cocktails; an à la carte restaurant that offers fine dining in an unpretentious relaxed atmosphere; and a basement club where you can dance the night away to live bands and DJs.

bluu

booly mardy's

What's in a name? Originally called Bloody Mary's, the name of these premises was the subject of a trademark dispute involving a rival. Known citywide to their faithful clientele as Bloody Mary's, the dispute became something of a cause célèbre in the city's press and customers were asked for their suggestions for a new name. The result was an anagrammatic name change to Booly Mardy's. Whatever the name may be, this West-End bar and restaurant offers an unrivalled selection of cocktails together with an extensive menu serving everything from light snacks to à la carte meals.

Louisiana Sunburst Salad
With Warm Cajun Chicken

2 chicken fillets, skin removed

2 tbsp Cajun spice powder

2 oranges

a handful of grapes

1 fresh pineapple, peeled, cored and diced

1 passion fruit, sliced

1 bag of mixed salad leaves

1 red pepper

1 white onion

1 red onion

½ cucumber

2 spring onions

25ml olive oil

salt and black pepper, to taste

4 strawberries, to garnish

Cover the chicken fillets in the Cajun spices and cook in the oven on a medium heat (180°C) for approximately 30 minutes.

Peel and segment one of the oranges and put the segments in a bowl with the grapes, pineapple, passion fruit and salad leaves and mix well.

Chop the red pepper, onions and cucumber and add to the fruit and salad mixture.

Slice the cooked chicken and toss the slices with the fruit and vegetable salad mixture.

For the dressing, mix the juice of the remaining orange with the olive oil, season to taste and whisk together.

To serve, pour the dressing over the salad and garnish with fanned strawberries.

Shredded Duck
with Egg Noodles and Sesame Seeds

50ml chicken stock
500g egg noodles
20ml sesame oil
1 large duck breast, skin removed and thinly
  sliced
½ yellow pepper
½ red pepper

2 spring onions
½ red onion
1 small piece of fresh ginger
a handful of fresh coriander
25ml dark soy sauce
1 tsp Chinese five-spice powder
a sprinkle of sesame seeds

Bring the chicken stock to the boil, remove the pan from the heat and soak the egg noodles for 5–10 minutes, until soft.

Heat the sesame oil in a wok and brown the sliced duck breast.

Meanwhile slice the peppers, one of the spring onions and the red onion. Peel and dice the ginger.

Add all the vegetables, ginger and the coriander to the wok containing the duck. Stir-fry for 2–3 minutes then add the drained noodles, five-spice powder and soy sauce.

To serve, put contents of the wok into a bowl and garnish with the other spring onion (shredded) and sprinkle over a few sesame seeds.

Seared Scallops,
Basil Creamed Leeks and Crispy Serrano Ham

4 slices of Serrano ham
1 medium leek
2 splashes of olive oil
250ml white wine
150ml double cream

salt and pepper, to taste
20 scallops, muscles and corals removed
8 basil leaves, torn
some chopped fresh chives, to garnish

Preheat oven to 180°C.

Put the Serrano ham on a non-stick baking tray and roast in the oven for approximately 5 minutes until crispy. Once cool, break each slice into 4.

Half and quarter the leek lengthways and finely chop it. Sauté the leek at a moderate heat in a frying pan with a splash of olive oil but do not colour them. Add the wine and reduce by half. Then add the cream and reduce by a quarter, season to taste and set aside.

Preheat a frying pan, add a splash of olive oil and sear the scallops for 1½ minutes on each side.

Add the basil to the leek, wine and cream sauce and gently reheat it.

To serve, pour the sauce directly on to the plates, place five scallops on each plate and scatter the pieces of Serrano ham on top, garnishing with the fresh chives.

Honey and Ginger Cheesecake

80g unsalted butter
30ml runny honey
400g ginger snap biscuits
500ml double cream

1kg Philadelphia or other soft cream cheese
200g white chocolate
150ml runny honey
a few sprigs of mint, to garnish

Heat the butter and the 30ml of honey over a low heat until melted.

Put the ginger snaps in a food processor and process them until they resemble breadcrumbs. Add the melted butter and honey mixture and combine it with the biscuit crumbs. Press the mixture into a cheesecake tin or a round cake tin (ideally one with a Springform base). Chill for at least twenty minutes.

Whisk the double cream until lightly whipped and put it in the fridge.

Put the Philadelphia cheese in a mixing bowl and beat it until soft. Melt the chocolate and add it to the cheese together with the remaining honey, mix this together and then fold in the lightly whipped cream. Pour the mixture into the cheesecake or cake tin and refrigerate for 3–4 hours or overnight.

To serve, remove the cheesecake from the tin, cut into portions and garnish with the mint sprigs.

Serves 10

Café Andaluz is an authentic Spanish tapas restaurant that uses a mixture of fresh local ingredients and imported Spanish delicacies to create a grand culinary experience with an array of traditional and modern tapas. Why not share tapas and make a meal of them or enjoy them as the prelude to traditional Andalucian paella? At Café Andaluz, the tapas experience goes hand in hand with hospitality, friendship and conversation.

café andaluz

As well as the stunning food, Café Gandolfi is famed for its Tim Stead furniture and John Clark's stained glass windows. A landmark restaurant, resident in the Merchant City for over twenty-five years, it specialises in the best of Scottish produce with a European flavour. Owner Seumas MacInnes is proud of 'Scotland's fantastic raw materials – from seafood to turnips'! And, upstairs, Bar Gandolfi is the perfect setting for rounding off the evening with after-dinner refreshments.

café gandolfi

Roast Rack of Lamb

with Olives, Thyme and Parsley

50g black olives, pitted
2 tbsp fresh thyme leaves
2 tbsp parsley
7 tbsp olive oil

4 cloves of new season's garlic, peeled
salt and black pepper, to taste
2 racks of lamb, approx. 500g each

Put the olives, thyme leaves, parsley, olive oil and garlic into a food processor and season with salt and black pepper.

Blitz the mixture and scrape it into a dish large enough to take both racks of lamb.

Roll the lamb in the paste, cover with cling film and set aside to marinade for at least 2–3 hours.

Preheat the oven to 220°C.

Transfer the lamb to a roasting tin or shallow ovenproof dish, spreading the marinade paste all over the meat. Roast for 25 minutes, which will toast the outside without burning the thyme and parsley and leave the flesh pink.

Remove the lamb from the oven and leave it to rest for a few minutes before serving.

This is delicious served with gratin dauphinoise, made by layering potatoes and leeks with Swiss cheese and cream, and some French beans.

Apple Brown Betty

for the topping
50g butter
150g fresh breadcrumbs
50g brown sugar
2 tsp ground cinnamon
1 tsp mixed spice

for the apples
1.6kg Bramley apples, peeled, cored and sliced
25g butter
150g sugar

crème fraîche, to serve

Heat the butter for the topping in a shallow heavy-based pan, add the breadcrumbs and stir continuously over a medium heat until they become crisp. When they are golden brown, remove them from the heat and stir in the sugar and spices. Set the mixture aside to cool.

Place the apples in a heavy-based stainless steel pan with the butter, a splash of water and the sugar and heat gently. Cover with a lid and stir occasionally. After 10–15 minutes, remove from the heat, ensuring the apples do not become too sweet as they should retain their inherent sharpness.

Serve the warm apple in bowls sprinkled with a generous amount of the topping and crème fraîche.

Vietnamese Rice Paper Rolls

50g mooli (white radish), cut into thin strips
50g carrot, cut into thin strips
50g onion, cut into thin strips
50g cabbage, cut into thin strips
2 tbsp vegetable oil
salt and pepper
50g sweet potato, peeled and grated
30g glass noodles
50g tofu (1 block), sliced
500ml vegetable oil for deep-frying
a pinch of granulated sugar

15g peanuts, crushed and roasted
5g sesame seeds, roasted
8 sheets rice paper
8 leaves butter leaf lettuce
30g fresh herbs – basil, coriander, mint –
  chopped
5g fresh ginger, grated
a pinch of granulated sugar
120ml soy sauce
20g mixed leaves

In a wok, stir-fry the strips of mooli, carrot, onion and cabbage in the oil, season and cool.

Deep-fry the sweet potato, glass noodles and tofu separately, until they are crispy, and then mix them all together.

Now combine the deep-fried and stir-fried ingredients and season with salt and pepper, sugar, peanuts and sesame seeds.

Soften the rice paper by dipping it in hot water for a few seconds. Drain it and lay it out on a flat surface. Top each sheet with a lettuce leaf, 2 tsp of the fried vegetable and tofu mixture and some of the mixed herbs. Roll up the mixture tightly in the rice paper, taking care not to rip it, to form a sausage shape. Slice each roll in half diagonally.

Mix the grated ginger and sugar into the soy sauce and divide this between 4 small shallow dishes or ramekins.

Serve 4 halves to a portion, along with a dish of the ginger, sugar and soy sauce mixture and a few mixed leaves.

Hunan Tiger Prawns

20ml peanut oil
50g red onion, sliced
50g bell peppers, de-seeded and cut into large
  dice
50g button mushrooms, quartered
50g mange tout
5g garlic, crushed
32 (about 600g) tiger prawns
60ml ready-made spicy soy bean paste

30ml ready-made oyster sauce
20ml soy sauce
30g pak choy
10g sesame seeds, roasted
500g jasmine rice, steamed and divided
  between 4 small bowls
30g spring onion, sliced
2 small shallots, finely sliced and fried

Stir-fry the vegetables and garlic in the peanut oil in a hot wok for 1 minute. Add the tiger prawns and cook for a further minute. Add the spicy soy bean paste, oyster sauce and soy sauce and continue to cook until the prawns are ready. Finally, add the pak choy, stir it in and cook for another 20 seconds.

Put the bowls of steamed jasmine rice upside down on each plate and remove the bowls. Arrange the prawns and vegetables around the rice and sprinkle the sesame seeds over them.

Finally, garnish the rice with the spring onion and fried shallots.

café mao

This Irish mini-chain opened its Glasgow outpost around six years ago. Since then, Café Mao has become a Merchant City landmark, famed for its outsized Warhol prints as well as for its excellent Asian fusion food. Café Mao offers a wide variety of menus and has intriguing drinks lists. With the infectious energy of its staff and the stylishness of its surroundings, it makes an ideal venue for couples and large parties alike.

Camerons offers a return to classic standards in dining. It skilfully achieves the elusive status of an intimate restaurant within a landmark city-centre hotel. The restaurant serves contemporary international cuisine using the freshest of Scottish produce. Many patrons are regulars who readily return to enjoy the friendly, yet discreet, service and innovative modern food.

camerons

Lemon Grass Marinated Sole and Sea Trout Roulade

with Young Vegetables, Potato Cake and Parsley Foam

4 x 140g fillets lemon sole
4 thin slices of sea trout, about 60g each

for the marinade
100ml olive oil
2 tbsp white wine vinegar
1 clove of garlic
zest of 1 lemon
1 stem of lemon grass, chopped
salt and pepper, to taste

for the spinach
250g young spinach
6 slices of truffle, halved
12 sprigs of chervil, chopped
4 sprigs of flat-leaf parsley, chopped

for the vegetables
4 baby carrots
4 baby beetroot
4 baby asparagus

4 baby courgettes
4 whole carrots, shaved into long strips on a
   mandolin
50g butter
salt and pepper

for the potato cake
250g mashed potato
6 sorrel leaves, chopped
50g shallots, chopped
salt and pepper
2 egg yolks
100g fresh white breadcrumbs
2 whole eggs, beaten
50g butter

for the parsley foam
100g flat parsley
4 tbsp double cream
100ml fish stock
50g butter

Mix all the marinade ingredients together, spread this mixture on the sole and trout and marinate for 4–5 hours. Slightly scrape off the mixture and place a slice of sea trout in the middle of each fillet of lemon sole, roll the fish up using cling film. When ready to cook, steam the 4 roulades for 6–8 minutes, remove the cling film and keep them warm till needed.

Boil or steam the spinach until just wilted and stir in the truffle, chervil and parsley.

To prepare the vegetables, cook them all separately until crisp. Toss them in the 50g of butter and season with salt and pepper to taste.

To make the potato cakes, combine all the ingredients, except the breadcrumbs, beaten eggs and butter, together to make 4 potato cakes and season them with the salt and pepper. Dip the cakes in the whole eggs and then in the breadcrumbs till they are coated and fry them in the butter until golden brown.

To make the parsley foam, blanch the parsley for 6 seconds in boiling water, remove and blend it with the cream and the fish stock using a hand blender. Put the mixture in a pan and heat until almost boiling (80°C). Add the butter and froth the mixture up with the hand blender.

To serve, cut each roulade into three pieces and place on top of the spinach. Add the vegetables and potato cake and pour the parsley foam around .

Côte de Boeuf (Rib of Beef),
Cherry Tomatoes and Potato Wedges

900g rib of beef, on the bone.
salt and pepper, to taste
olive oil
4 large cap mushrooms

2 small bunches cherry tomatoes on the vine,
 snipped into clusters of 3–4
3 large Maris Piper potatoes
a bunch of watercress

Preheat a frying pan with the olive oil. Season the beef and sear both sides until golden brown.

Put the beef on a baking tray to finish cooking in the oven at around 200°C – for medium rare, roast for about 10 minutes or, for well done, roast for about 20–25 minutes. Once cooked remove the meat from the oven and allow it to rest for 20 minutes before carving.

Pan-fry the mushrooms and cherry tomatoes in the pan used to sear the beef – the tomatoes take 2–3 minutes until the skin just starts to break while the mushrooms may need a little longer.

For the potato wedges, leave the skins on the potatoes and cut into wedges. Deep-fry them at a low temperature of around 140°C until soft, remove and set them aside. Just before serving, refry the wedges at 190°C until golden brown, sprinkling them with salt as soon as they are ready to keep them crisp.

To serve, arrange the carved beef, vegetables and potato wedges on a plate and put the bunch of watercress on top as a garnish. This can also be served with a Béarnaise, peppercorn or chasseur sauce.

Serves 2

Panna Cotta

600ml full-fat milk
600ml double cream
125g granulated sugar
2 vanilla pods, split

5 leaves of gelatine
a little butter
a selection of summer berries, to serve

Place the milk, cream, sugar and split vanilla pods into a pan and bring to the boil. Remove the pan from the heat straightaway, discard the vanilla pods and leave it to cool.

Soften the gelatine leaves in some lukewarm water for 5 minutes. Remove, squeeze out any excess water and dissolve it in the cream and milk mixture.

Lightly butter a mould so the dessert will turn out easily. (One large mould, several smaller ones, or ramekins or coffee cups could be used.)

When the panna cotta mixture is cool and close to setting, pour it into the mould(s) and allow it to set overnight.

Serve with a selection of summer berries.

Serves 10

This is the only place where you can see Sir Peter Blake's 'Alphabet' collection in all its glory. Gaze at works by the man behind the *Sgt Pepper's* album cover whilst enjoying classic dishes from the UK and Continental Europe. The informal but professional service is coupled with stylish decor and these are just two elements of Collage, which is based on a concept created by Roy Ackerman CBE.
As well as the à la carte menu, Collage offers daily specials and their signature 'One Plate' dishes. It also has a wine list specially designed for the restaurant by Joe Fattorini.

Collage

Cottier's

Cottier's restaurant is set in the Cottier's church building and the interior features the work of Daniel Cottier. The food draws inspiration from all over the world and classic dishes are the backbone of a menu offering an eclectic range that succeeds in being both interesting and familiar. The roasts are especially good.

King Scallops
with a Smoked Chipotle Salt on Chorizo Sausage with Coriander Pesto and Asparagus

1 tbsp sea salt flakes

1 tbsp lime zest

1 smoked chipotle chilli, deseeded, lightly
  roasted and blended to powder

1 tsp cracked black pepper

1 bunch of coriander

2 tbsp almond flakes

1 clove of garlic

1 tbsp Parmesan, grated

4 tbsp sunflower oil

salt and pepper, to taste

12 spears of asparagus, trimmed

12 slices of chorizo sausage

12 king scallops, with roe and muscle removed

Blend the salt, lime zest, chipotle chilli and pepper together and set the mixture aside.

To make the coriander pesto purée, combine the coriander, almond flakes, garlic, Parmesan and 3 tablespoons of the sunflower oil and season to taste.

Cook the asparagus by steaming the trimmed spears for 8–12 minutes.

Pan-fry the chorizo slices in a hot pan with no oil and set them aside.

Roll the edges of the scallops in the salt and chipotle mixture to coat them. Heat the remaining tablespoon of oil in a pan and when smoking hot add the scallops, a few at a time, and cook for 1–2 minutes each side until golden brown.

To serve, put a straight line of the coriander pesto on the plate, alternate the chorizo and asparagus to form a criss-cross pattern and place three scallops on the top of each.

Pappardelle Aragosta

2 whole lobsters, around 700g each
½ large onion, finely diced
2 cloves of garlic, puréed
8 large prawns, shelled and de-veined
1 good measure of brandy

1 small tin of San Marzano tomatoes
150ml double cream
8 basil leaves
salt and pepper, to taste
1kg pappardelle pasta

Place the lobsters in a large pan of boiling water and cook for 8–10 minutes until the shells turn bright orange. Remove them from the pan and put them in cold water. Allow the lobsters to cool then cut them in half lengthways and break open the claws. Put the lobsters in the fridge until you are ready to use them.

Place the diced onion, puréed garlic and prawns in a large, hot frying pan and slowly cook until the prawns are tender to the touch. Add the brandy and ignite the alcohol to burn it off. Then add the tomatoes and bring to the boil.

Add the lobsters to the pan and reduce the heat. Add the double cream and basil leaves and bring the sauce to a ribbon consistency. Add seasoning to taste.

Cook the pasta in a large pot of boiling salted water for 7–8 minutes until al dente.

Remove the lobsters from the tomato sauce and drain the pasta. Mix the pasta into the tomato sauce.

To serve, divide the pasta between 4 plates and top each with half a lobster.

Pizza Verdi

for the dough

1 small sachet of dried yeast

30ml extra virgin olive oil, plus a little more for
  coating

25g salt

450g '00' pizza flour

for the topping

1 small tin of San Marzano tomatoes

1 tbsp olive oil

1 mozzarella ball, grated

1 large packet of fresh spinach

1 small block of feta cheese, crumbled

1 small packet of rocket leaves

1 small piece of Parmesan cheese, shaved

1 small red chilli pepper, thinly sliced.

a pinch of salt

To make the dough, put tepid water in a large bowl and, following the packet ingredients, add the yeast. Leave for 3–4 minutes. Then slowly add the olive oil and season with the salt. Mix in the flour and knead into a ball. Lightly coat with olive oil, place a towel over the bowl and allow the dough to rest for 15 minutes.

Now separate the dough into 4 balls and leave for a further 10 minutes under a damp cloth. Stretch each of the dough balls into a round shape to form the pizza bases.

Spread the tinned tomatoes lightly on top of the pizza dough to cover it and drizzle with a small amount of olive oil.

Sprinkle over the grated mozzarella and add the spinach leaves and crumbled feta cheese, keeping back a few spinach leaves to use as a garnish.

Cook the assembled pizzas in the oven for 10 minutes at 220°–240°C.

When cooked, top the pizzas with the remainder of the spinach, rocket leaves, thinly sliced chilli and shaved Parmesan. Sprinkle with a pinch of salt.

di maggio's

Offering the very best in Italian–American cuisine, Di Maggio's is a Glasgow favourite. Family-run and serving great freshly prepared food, the restaurant takes great pride in the unique atmosphere it has created – an environment that everyone can enjoy. Whether celebrating a birthday, having a family meal or just grabbing a quick bite, enjoy the friendly service and great food.

firebird

Firebird is a busy local venue that uses organic and free-range products where possible. Child-friendly and with a healthy affordable menu, Firebird is the template of how a modern gastro-bar should be. The exceptional quality of the food and the intimacy of the atmosphere mean that, here, an evening with friends can turn into a night to remember.

yellow split pea soup

pork & leek sausages with mash & red wine jus £7.9⁵

whole roast flat fish with chilli butter & roast potatoes £6.9⁵

penne with chorizo, black olive & red onion £6.9⁵

coffee & croissant £2.5⁰

coffee & pain au chocolate £2.6⁰

black cherry tartlet with ice cream £4.2⁵

Fillet of Cod

with Orange-Cardamom Rice, Goma-Shio Crayfish Tails, Champagne, Lemon-Thyme and Saffron Sauce and Pistachio Oil

for the pistachio oil

75g good quality, very green pistachio nuts
100ml extra virgin olive oil

for the goma-shio crayfish

50g cooked seawater crayfish tails
1 tbsp black sesame seeds, lightly toasted
natural sea salt, to taste

for the orange-cardamom rice

280g Bali jasmine rice
720ml water
zest of 1 orange
6 cardamom pods, crushed

for the champagne, lemon-thyme and saffron sauce

4 shallots, sliced
50g butter
100ml champagne
100ml fish stock
100ml double cream
a pinch of saffron strands
4 sprigs lemon-thyme
salt and pepper, to taste
lemon juice

salt and freshly ground white pepper
4 x 200g fresh cod fillet, skin on
a little olive oil

To prepare the pistachio oil, put the pistachio nuts and the olive oil in a food processor and blend until smooth. Strain through a fine sieve and set the oil aside.

To prepare the goma-shio crayfish tails, simply mix them with the sesame seeds and salt.

Wash the rice thoroughly, soak in clear cold water for 10–15 minutes and then drain. Transfer it to a deep, heavy-based saucepan, add 720ml water, the orange zest and the cardamom pods. Cover, bring to the boil and cook over a high heat for about 5 minutes. Reduce the heat and simmer, still covered, for 10 minutes or until all the liquid has been absorbed. Remove from the heat, keeping the pan covered, and leave the rice to rest for a further 10–15 minutes.

To make the sauce, fry the shallots in the butter without allowing them to colour. Deglaze the pan with the champagne and reduce to a syrupy glaze. Add the fish stock, reduce again and then add the cream, saffron and lemon-thyme. Bring to the boil, then strain. Season and add the lemon juice to taste.

Season the fish and fry it in a little olive oil, skin side down, for 4 minutes, until the skin is golden and crisp, then turn it over and cook for a further 2 minutes until the fillets are just opaque.

To serve, place the fish and goma-shio crayfish tails on a plate, spoon the sauce over the fish, drizzle with the pistachio oil and serve with orange-cardamom rice.

gamba

If fresh seafood, such as lemon sole, halibut, monkfish or lobster, is to your taste, you will adore the superb cooking at Gamba. This award-winning stylish restaurant in Glasgow's city centre offers outstanding fresh and simple cuisine while the striking Mediterranean decor and excellent front-of-house service complete the experience.

Seared Fillet of Halibut

on a Stew of Smoked Haddock, Mussels and Asparagus with Avruga Caviar

500g mussels, cleaned

100ml white wine

2 large fillets of smoked haddock, preferably
  undyed

500ml double cream

4 halibut fillets

16 stalks of baby asparagus, blanched

1 small jar of Avruga caviar

a few chervil sprigs, to garnish

Cook the mussels in a covered pan until opened. Drain into a sieve over a bowl and set aside 100ml of the jus from the mussels. Once the mussels have cooled, remove them from the shells and set them aside.

Put the white wine and the 100ml of jus in a separate saucepan and reduce by two-thirds.

Remove the middle and side bones from the smoked haddock and cut the fish into chunks.

Add the double cream to the white wine reduction, bring to the boil and simmer for 1 minute.

Sear the halibut in a hot frying pan until coloured, then place under a medium grill for 4–5 minutes until cooked.

Add the asparagus, shelled mussels and smoked haddock to the cream sauce and simmer for 1–2 minutes until the haddock is cooked. Add 1 tablespoon of Avruga caviar to the mixture.

To serve, spoon the sauce on to the middle of 4 serving plates and place the halibut fillets on top. Garnish each with a sprig of chervil and a teaspoon of caviar.

Raspberry and Coconut Tart
with Raspberry Sorbet and Lemon Crème Fraîche

for the lemon crème fraîche
50ml crème fraîche
1 lemon
1 vanilla pod

for the pastry
250g plain flour
125g butter
60g of icing sugar
1 egg

for the filling
225g butter
225g castor sugar
4 eggs
30g plain flour
120g ground almonds
120g toasted desiccated coconut
1 punnet of fresh raspberries

for the sorbet
1kg fresh raspberries
4 tbsp honey
180g castor sugar
a pinch of salt

Mix the zest and juice from half of the lemon into the crème fraîche with the seeds from the vanilla pod and put the mixture in the fridge.

To make the pastry, rub the flour, butter and icing sugar together until it resembles breadcrumbs. Beat the egg and mix it in. Knead the mixture until a smooth paste is formed then leave to rest in the fridge for 1–2 hours. Remove it from the fridge and let it soften slightly. Roll out the pastry to 5mm thickness and use to line a 27cm-diameter pastry case. Line the pastry with baking parchment and fill the case with baking beans. Bake in the oven for 35 minutes at 180°C. Remove the baking beans and bake for a further 10–15 minutes until golden.

For the filling, cream together the butter and sugar until smooth and pale then add the eggs one by one into the butter mix (adding them too quickly may cause the mixture to split).

Sieve the flour and ground almonds together and then fold them into the creamed mixture and add the toasted coconut.

Pour this mixture into the prepared pastry case and smooth out with a palette knife. Arrange the fresh raspberries regularly over the mix and press down by hand. Cook for 40–50 minutes at 180°C until golden.

To make the sorbet, liquidise the raspberries and pass them through a fine sieve into a bowl. Add the honey, sugar and salt. Churn in an ice cream machine and place in the freezer.

To serve, turn out of pastry case and cut to desired portion size. Place on serving plate with a spoonful of crème fraîche mix to the side and a scoop of sorbet on top of the crème fraîche.

the mariner

The Mariner is renowned for its Scottish cuisine and the flambé dishes cooked at your table. This award-winning restaurant offers its guests a warm, friendly and relaxed atmosphere in which to enjoy a truly memorable dining experience. Why not make a night of it and stay in one of the fully equipped bedrooms with spectacular views over the Clyde?

Salmon Gathering

for the salmon mousse
500g hot-smoked salmon
200ml cream
juice of 1 lemon
a sprig of dill, chopped
a sprig of parsley, chopped
salt and pepper, to taste

for the smoked salmon panna cotta
500ml double cream
50g crème fraîche
grated zest from ½ a lemon
2 sprigs of dill, chopped
2 sheets of gelatine, dissolved in water
salt and pepper, to taste
500g smoked salmon, diced

for the smoked salmon jelly
150ml strong fish stock
a pinch of saffron

2 sheets of gelatine, dissolved in water
250g smoked salmon, sliced thinly and
  chopped into small pieces

for the smoked salmon rillettes
250g duck fat
500g hot-smoked salmon
4 slices of smoked salmon
3 sprigs of chervil, chopped
a handful of dill, chopped

for the lemon oil
1 lemon
25ml good quality olive oil
a pinch of salt
a pinch of ground black pepper
salad leaves and a mixture of fresh herbs, to
  garnish

for the salmon mousse

Blitz the salmon until smooth, put it in a bowl and then add the cream, lemon juice, herbs and seasoning. Scoop the mixture into a piping bag. Pipe the mixture into moulds lined with cling film and chill for 2 hours.
Remove the mousses from the moulds and discard the cling film.

for the smoked salmon panna cotta

Heat the cream and crème fraîche, add the lemon zest and remove the pan from the heat. Add the chopped dill and gelatine sheets and season to taste.
Line moulds with the smoked salmon and pour in the cream mixture. Chill for 4 hours before removing the moulds.

for the smoked salmon jelly

Bring the fish stock to the boil, add the saffron and gelatine and then allow the liquid to cool for 2 minutes.
Pour the mixture into moulds so that they are about a quarter full and chill them for 30 minutes.

Place a few small pieces of smoked salmon on top of the mixture, pour in more of the liquid and chill again. Continue adding alternate layers of mixture and salmon pieces and chilling until the mould is full.

Remove the jellies from the moulds before serving.

for the smoked salmon rillettes

Heat the duck fat, add the hot-smoked salmon, cook for 3–4 minutes and then take the pan off the heat and allow it to cool.

Allow the duck fat to solidify slightly, flake the flesh, add the herbs and season to taste.

Place a slice of the smoked salmon on to a piece of cling film and put some of the hot-smoked salmon along the edge of the slice of salmon. Roll it up into a cylinder shape and twist the cling film at the ends to secure it. Repeat for the other slices and then put them in the fridge for 2–3 hours before removing the cling film.

for the lemon oil

Cut the lemon in half and squeeze the juice into a bowl, remove any pips and cover with the olive oil. Season with salt and pepper and stir well before use.

Serve the four salmon dishes with salad leaves, lemon oil and fresh herbs.

Roasted Loin of Roe Deer,
Caramelised Shallots and Stoved Potatoes with a Raspberry and Beetroot Sauce

25ml olive oil
3 sticks celery, finely diced
1 leek, finely diced
1 carrot, finely diced
1 onion, finely diced
3 litres game or veal stock
1 glass of red wine
6 fresh baby beetroots, cooked
1kg new potatoes

a bunch of chives, chopped
75g butter
8 large shallots, peeled
100g sugar
100ml water
4 x 200g pieces of loin of roe deer
½ a punnet of fresh raspberries
salt and pepper, to taste
a handful of fresh thyme or rosemary, chopped

Warm 2 tablespoons of the olive oil in a pan, add the celery, leek, carrot and onion and sauté on a low heat for 10 minutes. Add the stock, bring to the boil, reduce the heat and simmer for approximately 2 hours. Add the red wine and reduce the liquid by half.

Peel the beetroots then cut half of them into fine dice and the other half into bite-size pieces.

Boil the new potatoes in seasoned water until cooked. When they have cooled enough, crush them down using your hand and place on a roasting tray. Add the salt, pepper, chopped chives and 60g of the butter. Put the potatoes in a hot oven (200°C) for 6 minutes, until crispy and coloured, then arrange them in metal rings to shape them.

Place the shallots, sugar and 100ml of water in a small pan and caramelise the shallots by cooking gently in a little olive oil for 12–15 minutes.

Season the venison and then seal it in a hot pan with the remaining olive oil. Put it in the oven (180°C) and cook for 4–5 minutes until pink. Remove the meat from the oven and leave it to rest for 3–4 minutes before carving each piece into several slices.

Put the diced beetroot into the vegetable sauce, add the butter and stir until the sauce has thickened before adding the raspberries.

Heat up the remaining chunks of beetroot in a small pan.

To serve, put the potatoes in the centre of a plate, add the venison slices, the caramelised shallots and reheated beetroot then pour the sauce round the plate and garnish with some fresh herbs.

Halibut
with a Risotto of Fennel, Sun-Blushed Tomatoes, Basil and Parmesan with Fennel Cream Sauce

for the fennel sauce
50g onion, finely chopped
50g celery, finely chopped
350g fennel, finely chopped
75g unsalted butter
a pinch of salt
1 star anise
2 – 3 sprigs of thyme
1 bay leaf
a pinch of ground white pepper
150ml fish stock
250ml double cream

for the risotto
300ml chicken stock

300ml water
50g onion, chopped
1 clove of garlic, halved
50g fennel, diced
30g vegetable oil
100g Arborio rice
50ml double cream, whisked until stiff
25g Parmesan, grated
5g basil, chopped
75g sun-blushed tomatoes

a dash of olive oil
salt and pepper, to taste
4 x 125g halibut fillets

To make the fennel sauce, sauté the vegetables in the butter in a stainless steel pan with a pinch of salt for 5 minutes without allowing them to colour. Then add the star anise, thyme, bay leaf and a pinch of ground white pepper and sweat for a further 2 minutes.

Add the fish stock and cream, bring to the boil then reduce to a simmer and cook for 20–30 minutes until the fennel is completely cooked.

Using a stick blender, lightly blend the vegetables but not to a purée and then pass the mixture through a fine sieve using a ladle to push it. Sieve the mixture twice more but without using the ladle. Set the mixture aside.

To make the risotto, warm up the stock and water. In a separate pan, fry the onion, garlic and fennel in the oil for 2 minutes until translucent. Then add the rice, stir and fry for a further 2 minutes to seal the grains. Then gradually add the stock and water, reserving a little for the reheating stage, and continue to stir for 18 minutes or until the rice is cooked al dente. Once cooked, remove the risotto from the pan and set it aside to cool.

Preheat a non-stick pan and add a dash of olive oil. Season the halibut fillets and add them, skin side up, to the pan. Cook at a medium-high heat until golden (approximately 3 minutes) then turn and cook for a further minute on the other side.

Meanwhile, add a small amount of stock to your risotto and reheat it. Now add the whipped cream, Parmesan, chopped basil and sun-blushed tomatoes, taking care not to over-stir and break up the tomatoes.

Reheat the fennel sauce.

To serve, place a spoonful of risotto in the middle of the plate, sit the halibut on top of it and pour the fennel sauce round.

michael caines
at abode

In December 2005, Michael Caines' restaurant was launched at ABode, Glasgow, in the former Arthouse premises. This is the first Scottish restaurant for Michael Caines, one of Britain's most acclaimed chefs – his country-house hotel in Devon boasts two Michelin stars.

The stunning restaurant is designed to provide the perfect setting for modern European cuisine. With its own wine room and champagne bar, it offers a very special dining experience. Service comes with real style to create an experience to be savoured.

mother india

On numerous occasions, Glasgow has won
the accolade of curry capital of the UK.
Mother India is a jewel in this crown. Using
fresh herbs and plenty of originality, the
chefs create Indian dishes with particular flair.
There is a twenty-first-century approach to
the traditional Indian buffet and each dish is
prepared to individual requirements, with
plenty of choice for vegetarians.

Chicken Pulau
with Green Peas

3 tbsp sunflower oil
1 onion, chopped
10 black peppercorns
4 cloves
2 black cardamoms
1 cinnamon stick
1 tbsp cumin
4 cloves of garlic

1 tsp salt
2 whole green chillies
50g tinned tomatoes
4 medium-sized chicken thighs
770ml water
550g basmati rice
100g frozen peas, defrosted

Heat the oil in a heavy-based pot then fry the chopped onion for 2 minutes until soft, add the peppercorns, cloves, cardamoms, cinnamon stick and cumin. Cook together until caramelised then add the garlic, salt and green chillies and cook for a further 10 minutes.

Add the tomatoes and the chicken thighs and cook for 25 minutes or until the chicken is cooked through.

Add the water to the same pan, bring to the boil, then add the rice and continue to cook over a medium heat for 25 minutes or until the water has been absorbed.

Add the peas to the top of the pot, cover with tinfoil and a lid and cook over a very low heat for 15 minutes.

Lamb Shish Kebabs

500g minced lamb

1 small onion, finely chopped

1 small potato, grated and squeezed to remove
  excess water

50g breadcrumbs

3 green chillies, finely chopped

¾ tbsp salt

½ tbsp red chilli powder

½ tbsp ground cumin

20g fresh coriander

1 egg

3 tbsp vegetable oil

wooden skewers, soaked in cold water to
  prevent burning

Mix all of the ingredients, except the oil, together in a large bowl and put in the fridge for 1 hour.

Preheat the oven to 200°C and put the oil in a large shallow tray.

Shape the mince mixture into balls around the wooden skewers, put them on the tray and place it in the oven. Turn the skewers after 10 minutes and then cook for a further 20 minutes.

Steamed West Coast Mussels
with Black Bean and Pepper Sauce

3 tbsp salted black beans, roughly chopped

3 tbsp soy sauce

2 tbsp rice vinegar

a good pinch of cracked black pepper

120ml water

2 tbsp sesame oil

1 green bell pepper, finely chopped

1 red bell pepper, finely chopped

1 bunch spring onions, sliced (reserve 2 for garnishing)

4 cloves of garlic, finely chopped

20g fresh ginger, finely chopped

2kg mussels, cleaned

fresh crusty bread

To make the black bean and pepper sauce, combine the black beans, soy sauce, rice vinegar and cracked pepper together with the water and set the mixture aside.

Heat the sesame oil in a large pan. When hot, add the chopped peppers and spring onions and fry for 30 seconds. Then add the garlic, ginger and mussels and cook for a further 30 seconds.

Add the reserved black bean and pepper sauce and stir. Cover the pan and leave on a high heat for 3 minutes. Stir again once the mussels begin to open.

To serve, ladle the mussels into warm bowls with the bean and pepper sauce. Discard any mussels that have failed to open. Finely chop the remaining spring onions and garnish the mussels with them. Serve with the fresh crusty bread.

Pan-Fried Squid
with Mediterranean Salad, Crispy Pancetta and Basil Oil

500ml water

1 tbsp salt

50g basil

150ml olive oil

4 slices of pancetta

170g mixed salad leaves, such as radicchio,
  lollo rosso, oak leaf and endive

80g cucumber, peeled, deseeded and sliced

50g red onion, sliced

12 cherry tomatoes, halved

400g squid

salt and pepper, to taste

100g Parmesan shavings

Prepare the basil oil at least 1 hour in advance by heating 500 ml of water with 1 tablespoon of salt. Blanch the basil for 30 seconds then remove it. Blend the basil-infused water together with 100ml of the olive oil for 1 minute. Cover the basil and oil mixture and keep it refrigerated until required.

Preheat the oven to 220°C.

Place the pancetta on a baking sheet and lay another baking sheet on top to keep the slices flat. Cook for 12 minutes or until crisp, drain it on kitchen paper and leave it to cool. Then break the slices into small pieces and set them aside until required for the salad.

Put the mixed leaves, cucumber and red onion in a large bowl with the cherry tomato halves and 4 tablespoons of basil oil and toss so that everything is well coated. Divide the mixed salad between 4 serving plates.

Slit the squid along one side, open it out flat and score the inside to make a diamond pattern, taking care not to cut all the way through. Cut it into 5cm pieces.

Heat a pan with the olive oil over a high heat then add the squid. Move the fish around the pan constantly for 2 minutes or until it starts to colour and curl up. Season the squid to taste with salt and pepper.

To serve, arrange the squid on the dressed salad, top with the Parmesan shavings and pancetta pieces and drizzle more basil oil around the dish.

mussel inn

The Mussel Inn is owned and run by shellfish farmers who take pride in sourcing produce from only the finest suppliers. They serve fresh, top-quality shellfish and seafood dishes in a simple appetising manner, complemented by a carefully selected wine list. This, together with the informal, relaxed surroundings and experienced, friendly staff, means enjoyment is guaranteed.

papingo

Highly regarded by the Glasgow public, Papingo has a great reputation for excellent, friendly service and a consistent level of top-quality cooking. As well as an à la carte menu, which is available for all-day dining, there are fixed-price lunch and pre-theatre menus. The modern style of cuisine, using fresh local ingredients, offers an innovative range of poultry, seafood, beef and vegetarian dishes. One of Glasgow's long-standing quality restaurants, Papingo is a bright, atmospheric and inviting restaurant where you will always receive a warm welcome.

Goat's Cheese, Sage and Cranberry Filo Parcels
with Mulled Wine Syrup

for the parcels

4 large sheets of filo pastry
200g goat's cheese, cut in thick slices
50g butter, melted
1 packet of fresh sage, chopped
1 small jar of cranberry sauce

for the syrup

275ml red wine
110g Demerara sugar
1 small piece of peeled root ginger
1 cinnamon stick
zest of 1 orange

Preheat the oven to 200°C.

Cut each sheet of the filo pastry into 15cm squares and the slices of goat's cheese into quarters. Take one piece of filo pastry, pour a little melted butter in the centre then sprinkle some chopped sage on to the pastry. Place another piece of pastry on top and put a piece of goat's cheese in the centre of the pastry and spoon 1 teaspoon of cranberry sauce on top of the goat's cheese. Lift up the corners of the pastry, draw them together and twist them to form a seal. Brush a little butter on top of the parcel.

Repeat this process for each parcel.

Put the parcels on a baking tray and cook in the oven for 10–15 minutes.

To prepare the syrup, put all the syrup ingredients into a pan, stir and reduce by half. Add seasoning to taste, allow the syrup to cool, strain it and set it aside.

To serve, place a parcel on each plate and spoon around the mulled wine syrup.

Turbot
with Baby Spinach, Gruyère Cheese and Spring Onion Glaze

450g baby spinach
50g butter
salt and pepper, to taste
a pinch of nutmeg
275ml double cream

75g gruyère cheese, grated
1 bunch spring onions, finely chopped
3 egg yolks
4 x 200g turbot fillets

Quickly wilt the spinach in a hot pan with half the butter and season it with salt, pepper and nutmeg. Remove the pan from the heat and keep the spinach warm.

Semi-whip the cream, add the cheese, spring onions, egg yolks and seasoning and set the mixture aside.

Grill the turbot fillets under a medium heat for 5–6 minutes on each side until just undercooked as it will continue to cook when removed from the heat.

Put an equal amount of warm spinach in the centre of 4 warm plates, place the turbot on top of the spinach and spoon the cheese glaze over the turbot.

Put the plates under the grill until the glaze turns golden brown and serve.

Scallops and King Prawns à la Sorrentina

a splash of extra virgin olive oil
1 clove of garlic, finely chopped
3 red chillies, deseeded and finely chopped
1 red pepper, deseeded and finely chopped
1 yellow pepper, deseeded and finely chopped
16 scallops, corals and muscles removed

16 king prawns
150ml white wine
12 cherry tomatoes, halved
25g fresh oregano, finely chopped
25g fresh basil, finely chopped
a bunch of wild rocket leaves, to garnish

Heat the olive oil in a frying pan and gently fry the garlic, chillies and peppers for 5 minutes until soft but not coloured.
Add the scallops and king prawns to the pan and cook for 1–2 minutes on each side.

Add the white wine to deglaze the pan and boil for 2–3 minutes then stir in the cherry tomatoes and herbs and allow them to heat through. Garnish the fish with wild rocket leaves.

This is best served with saffron rice blended with a selection of sautéed vegetables, such as courgettes, peppers and onions.

planet uno

Welcome to the real world of Mediterranean cuisine. Planet Uno is Glasgow's newest and finest Italian and Mediterranean restaurant and bar. Designed to provide a very comfortable yet modern environment, Planet Uno has a warm friendly atmosphere. On the menu, you'll find a wide range of traditional and contemporary Italian dishes, including freshly baked pizzas and homemade pasta dishes.

The restaurant also offers a 'Dining and Dance' experience with live music every Friday and Saturday evening.

rogano

Food fashions come and go but Rogano Restaurant retains what it has always stood for – luxury, elegance and serving the finest fish and seafood. Salmon, langoustines, scallops, lobster, halibut and oysters are all faultlessly prepared and presented in classic styles. And, with its fresh and original menu and long opening hours, Café Rogano is ideal for lunch after a shopping trip, meeting friends or a pre or post-theatre supper.

Roast Halibut
with Langoustines and Spinach Gateaux and Shallot Vierge

salt and pepper, to taste
4 x 200g halibut steaks
25ml extra virgin olive oil
20 small langoustines
500g picked spinach
salt and cracked white pepper, to taste

¼ of a freshly grated nutmeg
2 shallots, finely chopped
25ml extra virgin olive oil
10ml white balsamic vinegar
10g chervil, finely chopped
10g dill, finely chopped

Preheat the oven to 180°C.

Season the halibut steaks and shallow-fry them in hot olive oil for 30 seconds on each side then put them on a tray and cook in the oven for 12 minutes.

Poach the langoustines in water for 6 minutes. Reserve 4 for garnishing and shell the remainder for the gateaux.

Steam the spinach and season it well with salt, pepper and nutmeg.

Using individual timbale moulds, make the gateaux by pressing the langoustines and spinach mixture in alternate layers.

Sauté the shallots gently with the olive oil and until soft then add the white balsamic vinegar and the chopped chervil and dill to make the shallot vierge.

To serve, place the halibut steaks on the centre of the plate along with one of the gateaux and spoon around some of the shallot vierge.

Tia Maria Brownies
with Whipped Mascarpone and Chocolate Sauce

for the brownies

125g unsalted butter

125g castor sugar

2 eggs

150g self-raising flour

10g plain flour

40g cocoa powder

50g dark chocolate buttons

50g hazelnuts, peeled and slightly crushed

35ml Tia Maria

for the whipped mascarpone

250ml double cream

200g mascarpone cheese

20g icing sugar

for the chocolate sauce

100g unsalted butter

150g dark chocolate buttons

100ml double cream

150 ml milk

50 ml Tia Maria

Preheat the oven to 180°C.

To make the brownies, cream the butter and sugar together in a bowl until pale and fluffy, add the eggs and mix well.
Then add the flours and cocoa powder and mix to a paste.

Add the chocolate, hazelnuts and Tia Maria and mix thoroughly.

Line a 20cm baking tray with greaseproof paper, spread the mixture evenly and then bake in the oven for 25–30 minutes.

To make the whipped mascarpone, place all the ingredients in a bowl and whip until stiff.

To make the sauce, melt the butter and chocolate together.

In a separate pan bring the cream, milk and Tia Maria to the boil, pour the cream mix into the melted chocolate and butter, whisk everything together and allow the mixture to cool.

Martini of Citrus Tiger Prawns
with a Roast Pepper and Cherry Tomato Salad

24 tiger prawns, shelled, halved and cleaned

25g butter

4 shots of Martini vermouth

zest and juice of 4 limes

2 red peppers, finely chopped

2 yellow peppers, finely chopped

16 cherry tomatoes

60g capers

60g anchovies

240ml mayonnaise

In a frying pan, sauté the prawns with the butter and Martini.

Pour the lime juice and zest on to the prawns and leave to cool.

Sauté the peppers and tomatoes and leave them to cool.

Chop the capers and anchovies and mix them into the mayonnaise.

To serve, place the peppers and cherry tomatoes in a large Martini glass and top with the prawns. Finish with a spoonful of the mayonnaise.

strata

Strata is conveniently situated on Queen Street, adjacent to that hub of city life, George Square. Also close by are the Gallery of Modern Art and the lively shopping precincts of Argyle Street and Buchanan Street. The restaurant provides something for everyone – fabulous food, an enticing wine list, superlative cocktails and a funky atmosphere are all part of its special blend. Stunning modern design in a listed building setting ensures that this award-winning restaurant-bar is a firm Glasgow favourite.

stravaigin

Renowned in Glasgow and beyond for its wonderful food, its think-global-eat-local ethos and its quirky ambience, Stravaigin is one of the city's favourite restaurants. Throughout its ten-year history, the restaurant has developed and progressed its food to meet different tastes and trends whilst staying true to strong Scottish roots. An example of this is the fusion of a Chilean national dish, 'curanto' – a stew of seafood and meats – with Scottish mussels, langoustines, Argyllshire lamb and rabbit. Or why not try Scottish Aberdeen Angus sirloin topped with Cajun-style prawns or Smeeton's Farm lamb fillet with purple conga potatoes?

Roast Fillet of Cod
with Baked Beans, Crisp Potato Waffles and a Saffron Onion Purée

for the onion purée
2 tbsp olive oil
25g butter
2 Spanish onions, sliced
75ml double cream
a pinch of saffron
salt and pepper to taste

for the baked beans
1 Spanish onion, finely chopped
1 carrot, finely chopped
2 cloves of garlic, finely chopped
2 tsp freshly ground cumin seeds
2 tsp freshly ground coriander seeds
1 tsp paprika
2 tsp dried chilli flakes
2 tbsp olive oil

200g dried haricot beans, soaked overnight
 and parboiled
300ml tomato juice
100ml chicken stock
2 bay leaves
1 tbsp brown sugar
a splash of red wine vinegar
sea salt and cracked black pepper, to taste
2 tbsp parsley, freshly chopped
2 tbsp coriander, freshly chopped
juice of ½ a lemon

for the potato waffles
4 Maris Piper potatoes
2 egg whites
50g butter

a little extra oil for shallow-frying
4 x 200g cod fillets

To make the onion purée, heat 2 tablespoons of olive oil and 25g butter in a heavy based pan. Cook the sliced onions over a low heat for around 45 minutes, stirring frequently until they are golden brown.

Bring the double cream to the boil and infuse the saffron in it for 5–10 minutes. Combine the cream with the cooked onions and blend until smooth. Season to taste and set the purée aside, keeping it warm until required.

To make the baked beans, sauté the finely chopped onion, carrot and garlic with the spices and chilli flakes in the other 2 tablespoons of oil until soft. Add the haricot beans, tomato juice, chicken stock, bay leaves, sugar and vinegar. Season the mixture and transfer to a baking tray. Cover the tray with tinfoil and bake for around 30 minutes or until the liquid has been absorbed and the beans are tender. Add the chopped herbs and lemon juice to finish.

To make the potato waffles, cut each potato into 4 large chip shapes and, using a mandolin or peeler, slice them very thinly and mix into the seasoned egg whites. Criss-cross four slices of the potato to resemble a square, repeat with a second layer on top.

Melt the butter in a frying pan and cook the waffles until golden and crisp on the outside but soft in the centre. Preheat the oven to 200°C.

Heat a little oil in a frying pan and cook the cod fillets, skin side up, for 1 minute to seal, carefully flip the fish over and transfer it to the oven for 10–15 minutes or until cooked through.

To serve, spoon a little of the onion purée on to a plate and place the fish on top of it. Spoon a portion of beans alongside the fish and sit a potato waffle on top.

Peppered Venison Loin
with Kilkenny Croquettes and a Vanilla and Hendrick's Gin Sauce

for the sauce

1 tbsp olive oil
1 onion, roughly chopped
1 carrot, roughly chopped
1 leek, roughly chopped
4 cloves of garlic, roughly chopped
2 sprigs of rosemary
2 sprigs of thyme
2 bay leaves
6 juniper berries
1 vanilla pod
1 large glass of white wine
1 litre chicken stock
250ml double cream
35ml Hendrick's gin

for the croquettes

1 onion, finely chopped
4 cloves of garlic, sliced
25g butter
a splash of sunflower oil
½ a fresh nutmeg, grated
100g washed spinach
250g plain mashed potatoes
salt and pepper, to taste
breadcrumbs
egg wash

4 x 200g trimmed venison loins
roughly cracked peppercorns, to coat

To prepare the sauce, heat the olive oil and brown all the vegetables and the garlic in a large pan then add the rosemary, thyme, bay leaves and juniper. Split the vanilla pod, scrape the seeds into the pan and add the split pod too. Deglaze the pan with the wine and reduce until there is virtually no liquid left. Add the chicken stock and reduce by two thirds, add the cream and reduce again until it is the required consistency. Strain the sauce through a fine sieve, add the gin and keep it warm until ready to serve.

To make the croquettes, fry the onions and garlic in a little oil and butter, add the nutmeg, spinach and potatoes and mix thoroughly. Season to taste and set aside to cool.

When the mixture is cool, shape it into croquettes and roll them in the breadcrumbs, then dip them in the egg wash and then in the breadcrumbs again. These can be prepared in advance and kept chilled. To cook, deep-fry the croquettes for 3–5 minutes.

Coat the venison on the top and underside with the peppercorns to form a crust.

In a very hot pan, seal the venison for 3 minutes each side for rare, remove and rest for 1 minute. Increase the cooking times accordingly for medium or well done.

Slice the venison and serve immediately with the croquettes on the side and the sauce poured round.

Roast Organic Salmon

with Carrot Pappardelle, Grilled Fennel, Dill and Mustard Dressed Cucumber and Tomato Essence

2 large carrots, peeled and cut into thin strips
  using a mandolin
1 dstsp brown sugar
1 dstsp balsamic vinegar
1 tbsp olive oil
1 fennel bulb, peeled, trimmed and cut into
  6mm slices (reserve the fronds from the top of
  the bulb for garnishing)
salt and pepper, to taste
a squeeze of lemon juice
1 dstsp sugar

1 dstsp white wine vinegar
2 dstsp Dijon mustard
juice of ½ a lemon
1 dstsp dill, roughly chopped
black pepper, to taste
1 cucumber, peeled and cut lengthways
sea salt, to taste
6 plum tomatoes
4 x 200g organic salmon fillets with skin
50g butter, melted and seasoned with salt and
  pepper

Preheat the oven to 200°C.

In a large bowl, mix together the carrots, brown sugar and balsamic vinegar with a little olive oil, ensuring that the carrots are well coated. Layer the carrots thinly on a baking tray and bake in the oven for 20–30 minutes, stirring occasionally, or until they are succulent and tender. Set the carrots aside.

Season the fennel with salt, pepper, a squeeze of lemon and a touch of olive oil, then place under a hot grill and chargrill for a few minutes, turn and repeat on the other side and then set the fennel aside.

To make the dressing, dissolve the sugar in the white wine vinegar, mix in the mustard and the juice of ½ a lemon then whisk in 1 dessertspoon of olive oil. Maintaining an emulsion, continue whisking until glossy and thickened and the olive oil flavour begins to come through. Add the dill, season with black pepper and set aside.

Deseed the cucumber then cut into diagonal strips, place in a colander and season with sufficient sea salt to taste, mix well and allow to sit for an hour, then pat dry and set aside.

Process the plum tomatoes to a pulp and season to taste with salt, pepper and a little sugar. Place the pulp in a muslin-lined colander and collect the liquid that drains through and set aside.

Heat a large frying pan, add a little oil, coat the salmon fillets with the melted seasoned butter and place them skin side down in the pan. Allow the salmon to sizzle for a minute then place the fillets in an oven preheated to 250°c for 15–20 minutes or until cooked.

While the salmon is cooking, put the carrots and fennel in the oven to warm through.

When the salmon is almost cooked, flip the fish on to the flesh side and allow to rest whilst assembling the dish.

To serve, divide the fennel between 4 large bowls, put some carrot in each and then place the salmon on top of the carrot. Coat the cucumber with the mustard dressing and place it on top of the salmon, then pour on the tomato essence and drizzle the dish with olive oil. Sprinkle fennel fronds over the top to garnish.

stravaigin 2

Sharing the same passions, flair and ethos as Stravaigin, Stravaigin 2 adopts a more bistro-like approach to dining. This vibrant venue, situated off Byres Road in Glasgow's West End, is a little haven that's big on diversity. With the 'best burgers in Glasgow' sitting comfortably on the menu next to Hanoi duck, wonton crisps and citrus salsa, Stravaigin 2 admirably backs up the Stravaigin motto of 'think global, eat local'.

This informal Spanish restaurant bar specialises in tapas and paella with a contemporary twist. With a lively atmosphere and relaxed service, the restaurant offers a selection of authentic Spanish cooking, including daily specials, along with exclusively Spanish wines, beers and drinks. The concept was created by the celebrated chef, restaurateur and commentator on food from around the world, Roy Ackerman.

tapaell'ya

Roast Pork Belly
with Braised Chickpeas

500g pork belly
salt and pepper, to taste
enough olive oil for searing the meat
a sprig of rosemary, finely chopped
a sprig of thyme, finely chopped
2 cloves of garlic, finely chopped
a sprinkling of rock salt
1 tbsp marmalade, melted

for the chickpeas
200g chickpeas
1 red onion, diced
1 clove of garlic, finely chopped
a splash of olive oil
1 tsp cumin powder
1 tsp smoked paprika
100ml white wine
250g tinned tomatoes
salt and pepper, to taste

Preheat the oven to 200°C.

Season the pork belly with salt and pepper and sear it in a frying pan with the olive oil until golden brown. Set the meat aside and allow it to cool.

Put the pork on a baking tray, smother it with the finely chopped rosemary, thyme and garlic and sprinkle a few shards of rock salt over it.

Roast the pork in the oven for around 25 minutes until cooked.

Brush the top of the pork belly with the melted marmalade and glaze under a hot grill for 1 minute.

To prepare the chickpeas, soak them in 3 times their volume of water and leave overnight to absorb the water as they will become much softer and quicker and easier to cook.

Drain the chickpeas, put them in a saucepan, cover with salted water and bring to the boil, skimming off any scum that rises to the surface. Boil the chickpeas until they are soft (this could take up to 2½ hours), drain and set them aside.

Sauté the diced onion and chopped garlic in the olive oil until soft. Then add the cumin and smoked paprika powder, stirring quickly until cooked. Add the white wine to deglaze the pan and boil to reduce the liquid by half. Add the chopped tinned tomatoes, simmer for 30 minutes and then add the cooked chickpeas. Season to taste and cook for a further 30 minutes.

To serve, carve the pork into slices and serve with the braised chickpeas.

Crème Catalan

170g granulated sugar

900ml double cream

1 vanilla pod, split and with seeds retained

10 egg yolks

80g brown sugar

zest of 2 oranges

Preheat the oven to 180°C.

Put the cream and vanilla pod into a pan and bring it to the boil.

Whisk the egg yolks and sugar until they are pale, light and foamy.

Pour the hot cream mixture into the eggs and sugar, whisking all the time to prevent curdling. Remove the vanilla pod and add the orange zest.

Pour the mixture into individual ramekin dishes and place in a bain-marie (a baking tin filled with water) in the oven for around 45 minutes.

Remove the puddings from the bain-marie, allow them to cool and put them in the fridge overnight.

Sprinkle the brown sugar evenly over each crème Catalan and glaze either with a domestic blowtorch or under a hot grill.

Serves 6–8

Wild Arisaig Venison Cutlets
with Home-Grown Vegetables and Red Wine Gravy

1kg venison cutlets or loin, either 2 cutlets or
  200g per portion
salt and pepper, to taste
enough olive oil for searing the meat
500g home-grown beetroot
500g home-grown Chantenay carrots
a splash of olive oil
a splash of balsamic vinegar

100g butter
25g granulated sugar
300ml red wine
a handful of fresh thyme
a handful of fresh rosemary
2 tbsp redcurrant jelly
baby potatoes, boiled and kept warm

Preheat the oven to 220°C.

Season the venison and seal it in the olive oil in a hot frying pan. Transfer the meat to a roasting tray and then cook it in the oven for 6 minutes. Remove the venison from the pan and allow it to rest somewhere warm for 10 minutes.

In separate pans, parboil the beetroot and carrots with their skins on. After around 10 minutes, sparingly peel both but leave the tops on.

Transfer the beetroot to a roasting tray, drizzle with some olive oil and balsamic vinegar and cook it in the oven for 10 minutes.

Transfer the carrots to another roasting tray, dot them with 50g of the butter and a sprinkling of sugar and cook them in the oven for 10 minutes.

Return the pan that was used for the venison to the heat, pour in the red wine and add the thyme and rosemary.

Reduce the liquid by half and then thicken it with the redcurrant jelly. Discard the herbs and keep the wine gravy warm.

Crush the cooked baby potatoes with a fork, season them, add the remaining 50g of butter and then press them into a metal ring to shape them.

To serve, slice the loin or arrange cutlets on top of a potato cake, add the carrots and beetroot and pour the gravy around the dish.

At The Sisters you're guaranteed a sumptuous Sunday brunch or lunch. Bring the family or relax with friends and enjoy Scottish seafood platters or the roast of the day. Whether you fancy a light bite or a three-course meal, there's a great selection that includes our home-baked breads, oatcakes and delicious desserts.

The same menu and excellent service are available in both branches of The Sisters which are located at Jordanhill and Kelvingrove.

the sisters

two fat ladies

Two Fat Ladies, West End, is a renowned fish and shellfish restaurant in the heart of Glasgow. Located just yards from Kelvingrove Art Gallery and Museum and the University of Glasgow, this small informal restaurant is famed for its fish which is cooked with simplicity and care. Its reasonably priced menus offer great value for money and the compact wine list and friendly service add to the perfect eating-out experience.

A second Two Fat Ladies fish and seafood restaurant is now open in the city centre, providing the same quality of food and service.

Fillet of Cod
with a Polenta Crust Set on a Sun-Dried Tomato and Olive Crush with Pesto Dressing

16 new potatoes
8–10 pitted olives, roughly chopped
1 heaped tbsp sun-dried tomatoes
25g butter
salt and pepper, to taste
4 x 200g cod fillets
150g polenta

for the pesto
50g pine nuts
250g basil
250ml olive oil
50g Parmesan

Preheat oven to 180°C.

Boil the potatoes until cooked through, drain and allow to cool slightly then mix with the chopped olives, sun-dried tomatoes and the butter. Use a fork to roughly crush the mixture. Season to taste and keep the potatoes warm.

Cover the cod fillets on all surfaces with the polenta, add seasoning, place on a baking tray and put the fish in the oven for 8–10 minutes.

To make the pesto, toast the pine nuts in a dry non-stick pan for a minute then put them in a food processor with the basil, olive oil and Parmesan and blend to the desired consistency.

To serve, place a quarter of the potato crush on each plate, set a cod fillet on top of each mound of potato and drizzle some of the pesto dressing around.

King Prawns and Stir-Fried Greens
with Sweet-and-Sour Sauce

for the sauce

4 red peppers

a splash of olive oil

salt and pepper, to taste

1 large pineapple, peeled and cubed

2 cloves of garlic, crushed

1 large onion, roughly chopped

2 red chillies, chopped

200ml soy sauce

for the king prawns

20 large king prawns, peeled

20 small dots of butter

salt and pepper, to taste

for the greens

a splash of olive oil

100g mange tout

100g green beans

100g broccoli

a splash of soy sauce

To prepare the sauce, halve the peppers, deseed them and put them, skin side up, under a hot grill until the skin blisters and burns. Remove the peppers from the grill, leave to cool and then peel the skin off the peppers. Preheat a pan with a little olive oil and some salt and pepper. Do not allow the oil to smoke. Place all the sauce ingredients into the pan and stir, allowing the ingredients to brown slightly. Once browned set aside and allow to cool. When cool, put the mixture in a food processor and blend to produce an orangey-red sauce. Blend until the sauce reaches the desired consistency.

Put the prawns on a baking tray with a little butter on each prawn and sprinkle with salt and pepper. Grill gently for about a minute and a half on each side.

While the prawns are grilling, preheat a frying pan with some olive oil. When the oil is hot and smoking, stir-fry the greens with a little soy sauce for about two minutes. Do not overcook the greens as they should still be crunchy.

To serve, put some of the stir-fried greens on the centre of a plate. Pour some of the reheated sauce around the outside of the plate and place 5 of the prawns around each of the plates at regular intervals.

Calves' Liver
with Gin, Lime and Leeks

for the meat stock

1kg meat bones

275g vegetables (carrots, onions, celery and leeks), roughly chopped

100g bacon rind, roughly chopped

1 bunch of parsley, roughly chopped

1 tsp mixed peppercorns

4–5 pints of water

1 jar of redcurrant jelly

1 tsp salt

700g calves' liver, thinly sliced

salt and pepper, to taste

plain flour for dusting

25g butter

1 tsp olive oil

2 small leeks, chopped

3 measures of gin

4 tsp parsley, chopped

Preheat the oven to 240ºC.

First make the meat stock. Brown the bones and the vegetables in a hot oven for 30–40 minutes.

Put the browned bones and vegetables, bacon rind, parsley and peppercorns into a large pan and cover with water. Bring to the boil slowly and simmer for 3–4 hours. Check the stock regularly to remove any froth or scum which may rise to the surface.

Strain the stock and set it aside to cool. When completely cold, remove any fat that may have set on the surface.

Put the stock in a clean pot and boil it to reduce the liquid by half then add the redcurrant jelly and season to taste.

Season the liver on both sides with salt and pepper and then lightly dust it with the flour, shaking off any excess.

Heat a small amount of the butter in a large frying pan and, when hot, add half of the liver and sear it for 30 seconds on each side, remove to a warmed plate and repeat with the remainder of the liver.

Melt the remaining butter and olive oil in a pan, add the leeks, fry for 2–3 minutes and then add the gin and flame. Finally add the meat stock, season to taste, bring to the boil and add the liver. Cook the liver in the sauce for approximately 5–10 minutes, being careful not to overcook it.

To serve, place the liver on plates, add the leeks and the sauce and garnish with the chopped parsley.

Passion Fruit Crèmc Brûlée

7 egg yolks
105g granulated sugar
360ml milk
360ml double cream

1 vanilla pod (or 1 tsp vanilla essence)
6 ripe passion fruits
100g granulated sugar, for caramelising the top

Preheat the oven to 160°C.

Place the egg yolks and the 105g sugar in a bowl and whisk together until pale, smooth and fluffy. Set the mixture aside.

Mix the milk and cream, add the split vanilla pod or the vanilla essence, bring to the boil and set it aside to infuse.

Halve the passion fruits and remove the pulp to a sieve. Put the sieve over a bowl and push the pulp through with a spoon to make a purée.

Add the cream and milk mixture to the egg and sugar mixture and then add the passion fruit purée.

Pour the mixture into individual ramekins and bake in a bain-marie (a baking tin filled with water) for 35–45 minutes. Allow the puddings to cool.

Just before serving sprinkle the dishes with the 100g granulated sugar and glaze using a domestic blowtorch or under a very hot grill.

Serves 6–8

urban bar and brasserie

Opened in 2006, this restaurant occupies a landmark building in a prime city-centre location and has been refurbished to provide sophisticated and stylish surroundings. From the team behind the award-winning Gamba and Urban Grill restaurants, the menu reflects Derek Marshall's inimitable style of using the best-quality local ingredients to present classic dishes with a contemporary feel.

The large bar area provides the perfect place for a party and private dining facilities are also available.

Urban Grill offers top-quality all-day dining with a menu based around classic dishes prepared freshly and using only the best local produce. The restaurant regularly features live musicians on its baby grand piano and the bar area is open daily for cocktails, wines and beers as well as all-day light bites.

Opened in 2005, Urban Grill won two major industry awards within its first nine months of operation. Named as *The List's* 'Glasgow Newcomer of the Year', this was quickly followed by the accolade of being awarded 'Most Promising New Restaurant/Bar' in the Dram Scottish Licensed Trade Awards.

urban grill

Urban Grilled Lamb Chops
with Buttery Mash and Apple and Mint Jelly

for the apple and mint jelly
1kg castor sugar
1 litre water
1kg cooking apples
juice and zest of 1 lemon
100g mint, finely chopped

for the buttery mash
500g of potatoes, Red Roosters or Maris Pipers
100g unsalted butter
100ml double cream
salt and pepper, to taste

12 x 150g lamb chops, new season if available
salt and pepper, to taste
a little oil for brushing

The apple and mint jelly must be prepared in advance to allow chilling overnight.

To prepare the jelly, put the sugar and water in a large heavy pan and bring to the boil. Wash the apples and score the skin slightly then drop them into the boiling sugar and water. Reduce the heat to a gentle simmer and cook for 25 minutes.

Remove the apples with a slotted spoon and push them through a sieve into a bowl. Discard the seeds and skins then put the apple pulp back into the boiling sugar and water. Add the lemon juice and zest and boil to reduce the volume for 20–30 minutes.

Pour the jelly into a bowl and set it aside to cool. Now add the mint and put the bowl in the fridge to chill overnight.

Peel the potatoes and cook them until soft. Drain the water away, return the potatoes to the pan for 10 minutes to dry them off and then pass them through a sieve.

Boil the cream and butter together in a large pan, add to the mash and stir thoroughly. Season to taste and keep warm.

Season the lamb chops and lightly brush them with oil. Put the chops on a griddle pan or barbeque and cook for a few minutes each side.

To serve, put 2 chops on each plate, top with a teaspoon of the apple and mint jelly and serve with the buttery mash. Green beans wrapped in bacon would make the perfect vegetable dish to accompany this.

Serves 6

Smoked Salmon and Haddock Fishcakes
with Spicy Salsa Relish

for the fish cakes
400g potatoes, Red Roosters or Maris Pipers

200g peat-smoked haddock

150g sliced smoked salmon

1 good pinch of chopped chives

2 dstsp creamed horseradish

salt and pepper, to taste

100g plain flour

2 eggs, beaten

200g breadcrumbs

50g butter

a handful of fresh herbs (chervil and flat-leaf parsley work well) and lemon wedges to garnish

for the salsa
2 red peppers

6 plum tomatoes

1 onion

1 clove of garlic

a splash of olive oil

2 red chillies

1 large glass white wine

1 tbsp of castor sugar

1 bunch coriander, chopped

Preheat the oven to 180°C.

To prepare the fishcakes, peel the potatoes and cook them until soft. Drain the water away, return the potatoes to the pan for 10 minutes to dry them off and then mash them.

Poach the haddock in water until just cooked and drain off the water before flaking the fish.

Shred the smoked salmon and add both types of fish to the mashed potato.

Add the chives and horseradish, season to taste and then allow the mixture to cool. Once cool, divide it into 6 equal portions and mould them into cake shapes.

Coat the cakes in flour, then pass through the beaten egg mix and coat in breadcrumbs. Chill the fishcakes for 1 hour.

To prepare the salsa, quarter the peppers and grill them until their skins turn black. Remove them from the heat and place in a plastic bag or tub to cool. Once the peppers are cool, remove the skins and seeds and chop them into fine dice.

Remove the eyes from the tomatoes and make small crosses at each end. Blanch them in boiling water for a few seconds and then plunge them into ice-cold water. Remove the skin from the tomatoes, half them, discard the seeds and chop the flesh into small dice.

Finely dice the onion and garlic and fry in a little olive oil, until soft. Add the chillies, white wine and sugar and boil to reduce the liquid by half. Now add the tomatoes, peppers and chopped coriander. Set the salsa aside and keep it warm until required.

Gently fry the fish cakes in butter until golden brown and then put them in the oven for 10 minutes to cook through.

To serve, divide the salsa between 6 plates and place a warm fishcake on each. Garnish with fresh herbs and lemon wedges.

Serves 6

Sweet Potato Soup
with Curry and Coconut

40g butter
2 onions, chopped
4 cloves of garlic, chopped
a small piece of root ginger, peeled and
  chopped
1 tbsp curry powder
1 tbsp ground cumin
3 cardamom pods, crushed
1 tbsp ground coriander

2 tbsp tomato purée
6 large sweet potatoes, peeled and chopped
1.2 litres vegetable stock
½ tin of coconut milk
1 dstsp chilli jam
salt and pepper, to taste
2 tbsp desiccated coconut
crème fraîche (optional)

Melt the butter in a thick-bottomed pan, add the onions, garlic and root ginger and cook until slightly coloured.

Add the curry powder, ground cumin, crushed cardamom pods and ground coriander and cook for a further 5 minutes on a low heat, stirring occasionally.

Add the tomato purée, mix in the sweet potatoes and stir. Gradually add the vegetable stock, mixing all the time, bring to the boil. Reduce the heat and simmer for 30–45 minutes.

Add the coconut milk and chilli jam, season to taste and simmer for a further ten minutes.

Remove from the heat, liquidise the soup then add the desiccated coconut and set it aside to cool.

If possible, cook the soup a day in advance to allow the flavours to develop.

To serve, gently reheat the soup, adding crème fraîche if you like.

Prawn Cocktail and Pear Open Sandwich
on Rye Bread

for the Marie Rose sauce

8 tbsp mayonnaise

2 tbsp tomato ketchup

1 tbsp brandy

½ tsp Tabasco

½ tsp Worcestershire sauce

salt and pepper, to taste

250g frozen peeled prawns, defrosted overnight

1 cos lettuce, finely chopped

4 slices rye bread, plain or toasted

1 pear, quartered then sliced

1 lemon, cut into wedges

a small bunch of chives, chopped

Mix the mayonnaise, tomato ketchup, brandy, Tabasco and Worcestershire sauce in a large bowl and season to taste.

Combine the prawns with the Marie Rose sauce, add the cos lettuce and mix thoroughly.

Put the prawn mixture on the bread, top it with the pear slices and serve garnished with the lemon wedges and chopped chives.

vroni's

In the heart of Glasgow's city centre, Vroni's wine and champagne bar offers the perfect atmosphere in which to relax and unwind after a hard day. Customers can select from extensive lists of champagne and wine or indulge in a cocktail. The light-dining menu provides the perfect sustenance with a range of soups, sandwiches, tapas and snacks.

windows

Situated on the seventh floor of the Carlton George Hotel, Windows is Glasgow's top dining experience. Windows has built a superb reputation for both the quality of its food – which is prepared using only the finest Scottish produce – and its professional and friendly service. These elements are matched by the stunning views over the city's rooftops.

Stuffed Chicken
with Smoked Salmon and Dill Mousse with Crushed Potatoes and Champagne Cream

for the salmon mousse
1 chicken fillet
100g smoked salmon
20g dill
1 egg white
salt and pepper
150ml double cream

4 chicken fillets

for the sauce
1 onion, sliced
1 clove of garlic, crushed
20g butter

100ml champagne
juice of 1 lemon
300ml double cream
salt and pepper, to taste

for the crushed potatoes
25 new potatoes
1 tbsp coarse-grain mustard
2 tbsp flat-leaf parsley, chopped
20g butter
salt and pepper, to taste

2 plum tomatoes

To make the salmon mousse, put the chicken fillet in a food processor along with the smoked salmon, most of the dill (keeping some for garnishing), the egg white and the seasoning and process until finely puréed. Slowly incorporate the cream, being careful not to over process as the mixture will split. Once everything is fully mixed, refrigerate for at least 1 hour.

Insert a thin-bladed knife into the rear of the remaining 4 chicken fillets and push down the length of them to create pockets. Put the chilled salmon mousse mixture into a piping bag and pipe the mousse into the pockets, cut the tips from the fillets and use them to plug the holes. Roll each fillet tightly in cling film and poach them for 12–14 minutes. Remove cling film and keep them warm.

To make the sauce, sauté the onion and garlic in the butter until soft. Add the champagne and lemon juice and reduce the liquid by half. Add the cream and seasoning, bring to the boil and whisk in the butter. Adjust seasoning as required. Cook the new potatoes in salted water. Once they are cooked, roughly mash them together with the mustard, parsley, butter and seasoning.

Skin and deseed the plum tomatoes and finely dice them.

To serve, slice each chicken fillet into three. Mould the crushed potatoes in the centre of the plate and arrange the chicken and sauce alternately around the plate. Garnish with the diced tomato and dill.

Gourmet Glasgow
food festival

weights, measures and servings

Standards Liquid

1 tsp	= 5ml
1 tbsp	= 15ml
1 fl.oz	= 30ml
1 pint	= 20 fl.oz
1 litre	= 35 fl.oz

Standards Solid

1 oz	= 30g
1 lb	= 16 oz
1g	= 0.35 oz
1 kg	= 2.2 lb

Liquid Conversions

Metric	Imperial
15ml	½ fl.oz
30ml	1 fl.oz
50ml	1⅔ fl.oz
100ml	3⅓ fl.oz
250ml	8 fl.oz
500ml	16 ⅔ fl.oz
600ml	20 fl.oz (1pint)
1 litre	1¾ pints

Solid Weight Conversions

Metric	Imperial
5g	⅙ oz
10g	⅓ oz
15g	½ oz
30g	1 oz
50g	1⅔ oz
60g	2 oz
90g	3 oz
100g	3⅓ oz
250g	8⅓ oz
500g	16⅔ oz

Oven Temperature Conversions

°C	Gas	°F
110	¼	225
120	½	250
140	1	275
150	2	300
160	3	325
175	4	350
190	5	375
200	6	400
220	7	425
230	8	450
240	9	475
260	10	500

All weights, measures and servings are approximate conversions and, because of this, mixtures of imperial and metric should not be used.

contributor details

78 St Vincent
78 St Vincent Street
Glasgow   G2 5UB
0141 248 7878
www.78stvincent.com

Arisaig
140 St Vincent Street
Glasgow   G2 5LA
0141 204 5300
www.arisaigrestaurant.com

Ashoka Ashton Lane
19 Ashton Lane
Glasgow   G12 8SJ
0800 195 3195
www.harlequinrestaurants.com

Aurora
Langs Hotel 2 Port Dundas Place
Glasgow   G2 3LD
0141 333 1500
www.langshotels.co.uk

Baby Grand West End
2 Byres Road
Glasgow   G12 3QA
0141 337 1145
www.babygrandglasgow.co.uk

Barca Tapas
Princes Square 48 Buchanan Street
Glasgow   G1 3JN
0141 248 6555
www.barcatapas.co.uk

Bluu
60 Trongate, Albion Street
Glasgow   G1 5EP
0141 548 1350
www.bluu.co.uk

Booly Mardy's
28 Vinicombe Street
Glasgow   G12 8BE
0141 560 8004
www.bloodymary.co.uk

Café Andaluz
2 Cresswell Lane
Glasgow   G12 8AA
0141 339 1111
13/15 St Vincent Place
Glasgow   G1 2DW
0141 222 2255
www.cafeandaluz.com

Café Gandolfi
64 Albion Street
Glasgow   G1 1NY
0141 552 6813
www.cafegandolfi.com

Café Mao
84 Brunswick Street
Glasgow   G1 1TD
0141 564 5161
www.cafemao.com

Camerons
Hilton Glasgow
1 William Street
Glasgow   G3 8HT
0141 204 5555
www.hilton.co.uk/glasgow

Collage
Radisson SAS Hotel
301 Argyle Street
Glasgow   G2 8DL
0141 225 2046
www.collagerestaurant.5pm. co.uk

Cottiers
93/95 Hyndland Road
Glasgow   G11 5PX
0141 357 5825

Di Maggio's
21 Royal Exchange Square
Glasgow   G1 3AJ
0141 248 2111
www.dimaggios.co.uk

Firebird
1321 Argyle Street
Glasgow   G3 8TL
0141 334 0594

Gamba
225a West George Street
Glasgow   G2 2ND
0141 572 0899
www.gamba.co.uk

The Mariner
Crowne Plaza Hotel
Congress Road
Glasgow   G3 8QT
0141 306 9988
www.ichotelsgroup.com

Michael Caines at ABode
ABode Glasgow
129 Bath Street
Glasgow   G2 2SZ
0141 572 6011
www.abodehotels.co.uk

Mother India
28 Westminster Terrace
Glasgow   G3 7RU
0141 221 1663

Mussel Inn
157 Hope Street
Glasgow   G2 2UQ
0141 572 1405
www.mussel-inn.com

Papingo
104 Bath Street
Glasgow   G2 2EN
0141 332 6678
www.papingo.co.uk

Planet Uno
122 Stockwell Street
Glasgow   G1 4LW
0141 552 8100
www.planet-uno.co.uk

Rogano
11 Exchange Place
Glasgow   G1 3AN
0141 248 4055
www.rogano.co.uk

Strata
45 Queen Street
Glasgow   G1 3EH
0141 221 1888
www.strataglasgow.com

Stravaigin
28 Gibson Street
Glasgow   G2 8NX
0141 334 2665
www.stravaigin.com

Stravaigin 2
8 Ruthven Lane
Glasgow   G12 9BG
0141 334 7156
www.stravaigin.com

TaPaell'Ya
Robertson Street
Glasgow   G2 8DL
0141 225 2047
www.tapaellya.5pm.co.uk

The Two Sisters
1a Ashwood Gardens, off Crow Road,
Glasgow G13 1NU
0141 434 1179
36 Kelvingrove Street
Glasgow   G3 7RZ
0141 564 1156
www.sistersrestaurant.com

Two Fat Ladies
88 Dumbarton Road
Glasgow   G11 6NX
0141 339 1944
118a Blythswood Street
Glasgow   G2 4EG
0141 847 0088

Urban Bar and Brasserie
23/25 St Vincent Place
Glasgow   G1 2DT
0141 248 5636/0141 572 0567
www.urbanbrasserie.co.uk

Urban Grill
61 Kilmarnock Road
Glasgow   G41 3YR
0141 649 2745
www.urbangrill.co.uk

Vroni's
47 West Nile Street
Glasgow   G1 2PT
0141 221 4677
www.vronis.co.uk

Windows
Carlton George Hotel
44 West George Street
Glasgow   G2 1DH
0141 354 5070
www.carltonhotels.co.uk

Recipe Index